In the Eyes of the Law

The True Story of Love, Betrayal, Murder, Fame and Justice in 1950's America

By

Tom Faulconer

ISBN: 0-7596-8834-6 (e-book)
ISBN: 0-7596-8835-4 (Paperback)
ISBN: 1-4033-3469-2 (Dustjacket)

This book is printed on acid free paper.

1stBooks - rev. 08/13/02

For my sister, Jackie.
She was here for the beginning,
but never saw the end.

To Lauralee + Peter—

Best Wishes!

Tom Faulconer

Acknowledgements

In researching and writing this book, I had the opportunity to take myself back to a time in my hometown not so different from what I remember growing up. But immersing myself in the Midwest in the 1950s would not have been possible without the help of others.

First and foremost, I would like to thank my father for his help. Luckily, even after 50 years of marriage, my parents have thrown very little away, so the access I had to his trial records and newspaper clippings was immeasurable. And, thanks to my mother for finding much of it!

Thanks also goes to the many people willing to discuss the case with me, especially Robert Penno who gave me insight into the trial that no one else could give, and Dr. Emmett Pierce for his keen memory.

Many people write books only to have them sit on the shelf and never see the light of day. This might well have been one of them, had it not been for the hope and guidance of Kathleen Purdum. Her expertise and contacts were invaluable and I will be forever grateful.

Thanks to my de facto editors (which could also mean unpaid): Lieutenant Steven Gibbs of the Marion County Sheriff's Department, and Gerry Danielson, among others.

My thanks to Lou Stoops, the Monday Morning Motivator, for steering me in the right direction.

Finally, to my family, Jeannie, T.J., Patty and Jodi.

Preface

True crime has always been a fascinating genre to me. I have been a devoted reader of this type of book for twenty years now. Plus, with cable and satellite television, coverage of infamous crimes has proliferated.

However, a few years ago, I began to wonder about some of the books I was reading. They routinely contained conversations between characters and other information that, to me, seemed very strange that the author would know firsthand. After reading a few prefaces more carefully, I discovered that not all was "true" in "true crime." Many of the best-selling authors admitted concocting scenes, conversations and employing other literary devices to "pad" their books and keep them interesting.

This revelation left me uneasy and suspicious. Suddenly, I wondered how much of what I was reading was actually true and how much was a fictional creation.

You might notice that the book you are holding in your hand is not as thick as many true crime works. And the reason is simple. Every bit of this story has been substantiated and documented by me, the author. This contains no "recreations" or literary devices based on what "might have" or "must have" happened. Every word in this book is true. Of that, I am very proud.

Certainly, and admittedly, there may be a slight inaccuracy or two. After all, it has been more than forty years since this story began. People die, memories fade. However, any inaccuracy is surely slight at best and of very little, if any, consequence to the story. And all of the information in this book came straight from people who were there.

Another reason not to introduce elements of fiction into a non-fiction book comes to mind. If an author has to make things up to keep the book interesting, perhaps he has chosen the wrong story. In this book, all of the elements were already present: love, adultery, stalking, murder, struggle, ambition, fame, wealth, justice and an engaging setting in the late 1950s.

Why would I need any more?

Chapter 1

"Many a tear has to fall, but it's all in the game...
Tommy Edwards
"It's All In The Game"
#2 song of 1958

The twentieth century had more than its quota of "Crimes of the Century." From the fall of Roscoe "Fatty" Arbuckle, one of the top actors in the early 1900s, to the kidnapping of the Lindbergh baby that riveted the world, to serial killers whose names became forever synonymous with insanity and death, every few years or so, the bar was raised and a new "Crime of the Century" was proclaimed.

A majority of people alive today know only one "Crime of the Century." Like the Titanic, the name O.J. Simpson once conjured greatness but in the blink of an eye, now means quite the opposite. What was once an acronym for greatness, success and the American dream now stands for everything that we view wrong with the American justice system.

Incredibly, the O.J. trial was televised every day. More amazingly, it was watched. Communications technology proved to be a double-edged sword, providing us instantaneous glimpses into the lives and problems of others, while slowly, methodically eroding our ability to be shocked by what we see.

What follows is a story that might take place today. But the reaction to it would be vastly different. In fact, we have become so desensitized that it might not even warrant space on the front page of most newspapers. But this story took place in a different time. A time when murder of the rich and powerful was still news. A time when the world was a different place.

1958 is unrecognizable by today's standards. Cuba was a favorite honeymoon destination and Fidel Castro was little more than an irritant to President Fulgencio Batista Zaldìvar. Rosa Parks had, after a tough day, perhaps inadvertently lit the fuse of civil rights that would guide much of our country's political process for decades. Yet "whites only" was a phrase that would still be common for years. And Cadillac was the undisputed symbol of success punctuated by tail fins that commanded dominance over "lesser" makes.

Most of all, this was still a time of innocence and optimism. Ike was in the White House and, as far as we knew, all was right with the world. The conservative workers bent on saving money for a rainy day, a philosophy born of the depression thirty years prior, were being replaced by younger, more flamboyant, more hedonistic workers. Camelot was experiencing its birth in a Massachusetts senator named Jack Kennedy, and although Vietnam was becoming a political preoccupation, the thought of the United States ever losing a war was ridiculous. We were still riding the economic tide of our World War II victory.

Certainly, crime was a problem in the highly populated areas, but the suburban sprawl crept further and further from the blight to former cornfields planted in rows of neatly lined houses with unlocked doors. Developers were finding the keys to success in the form of subdivisions. Young consumers were finding the manifestation of their success in the same places.

Perhaps this isn't a story that would shock the world today. But in 1958, it was called the "Crime of the Century." And, in a way, it was. The murder and trial that followed changed forever all of the Crimes of the Century that came later. When America turned on the O.J. trial, it was really watching a little bit of this story. In 1958, this story was appropriately uncommon. 40 years later, it is, shockingly, much too common.

But not everyone shared in the innocence and optimism that delineated the 1950s from the coming decades. Several people in Indianapolis, Indiana in the 1950s endured personal turbulence and struggle that would bring them together on the most unlikely of stages. And in the process, a nation would be mesmerized by their story.

Chapter 2

Rock and Roll…Sputniks…Flying Saucers…Now, EDSEL!
Sign on Ford Dealership
1958

Indianapolis, Indiana was, in many ways, an idyllic city in 1958. And the area around East 38th Street and Meadows Drive was a microcosm of that idealism.

38th Street formed the southern edge of an area, somewhat ironically, called The Meadows. The name was particularly ironic because, even though it had once been a meadow, the meadow had been replaced by the steel, concrete, brick and asphalt that now bore its name. There wasn't a meadow in sight of The Meadows.

Times were changing rapidly in Indianapolis and The Meadows was a sign of those times. Most Indianapolis residents had grown up completing routine errands as passengers on the interurban streetcars and still couldn't get used to riding bulbous, smoke-belching Indianapolis Transit buses instead. The first real shopping *mall,* Glendale Mall is minor league compared to malls today. It didn't even have a roof over it until the late 1960's. But it was the first of many to come and signaled the first shot in the revolution of the shopping experience in Indianapolis. Still, a die-hard shopper would rather go downtown to multi-story L.S. Ayres and Blocks Department Stores with their tea rooms and elevator operators. More than a few women still wore hats and white gloves to go shopping.

African-Americans, still formally called Negroes by politicians and even themselves were finally making inroads to the white culture that still dominated society all across America. *Brown vs. Board of Education*, the U.S. Supreme Court decision that ordered desegregation of government funded schools was just two years old, and some cheered, others shuddered when Althea Gibson, a young, black tennis player, outlasted all of the white contestants in the Tennis Championships in Wimbledon, England. With the recent integration of baseball, many Americans viewed tennis and golf as the last of the "white people's" games.

The Meadows was really an experiment in suburban living. The premise was simple: people could live, work and play all in the same place. The Meadows consisted of several apartment buildings, housing subdivisions, a shopping center that in today's vernacular would be called a "strip center," office buildings and places for entertainment. All of this was carefully planned and built in a square mile of, what was then, the outer suburbs of Indianapolis.

As it turned out, the timing of the development of The Meadows was quite fortuitous. Many of the GIs from World War II had finished college on the GI bill a few years earlier and decided to make the area around 38th Street their home. The homes and apartments were newer and better appointed than the homes their parents had lived in and the eclectic mix of shopping and entertainment literally steps away was too attractive for many young singles and couples to ignore.

The Meadows was the place to live in the 50's and 60's in Indianapolis.

But like many social experiments, over time this one went bad. In 1958, crime in the Meadows was rare. It was the place to live for young professionals long before they were known by that moniker. But by the end of the 1980s, The Meadows was one of the most dangerous places in Indianapolis. The apartments had become government housing. The shopping mall had one lone tenant, a beauty supply store, and all but the most die-hard of businesses had left. White picket fences had been replaced by chain link eight feet tall, topped with barbed wire and shackled with padlocks coldly foretelling visitors of the danger nearby.

By the end of the twentieth century, The Meadows was certainly not a place any person would choose to go. Its residents lived there by circumstance, not by choice.

But 40 years ago, when The Meadows was a magnet for young families, white collar and blue-collar workers alike, the sight of a brand new, long white Cadillac, while it might turn a head or two, wasn't something that would cause an extraordinary reaction.

For several minutes, the Cadillac had sat, parallel parked across the street from the first apartment building west of Meadows Drive on a street that snaked through the Meadowbrook apartments called 39th Street. Although the numbered street gave the impression of a major thoroughfare, being just one block from 38th Street, an essential artery in Indianapolis to this day, in truth, it was simply a driveway into and out of the apartments.

The apartment building that loomed over the silent Cadillac was identical to all the others in the complex. It was constructed of a brownish-red brick, three stories tall, with the first story in a half-basement such that those occupants on the first floor lived below grade, but had "average" sized windows that let the natural light in. Visitors and residents entered the buildings by climbing a few steps that rose to a doorway. Behind the door was the second floor of the building. One could stay on that floor, or take the stairs up a flight or down a flight. The footprint of each building looked like an I-beam positioned parallel to the street with two entryways just inside the indentation. 12 apartments, 4 per floor, two on each side, were accessible from each entry by their own respective doors.

The building had no elevators or ramps, being built long before the needs of the elderly and handicapped were a concern.

The mere passing of the new Cadillac would not have caused more than a few looks in the Meadowbrook apartment complex that evening. Yet at 1 AM on July 31,

1958, in the parking lot of the Meadowbrook Shopping Center, engulfed in the near total quiet that had descended over the several hours since most of the stores had closed for the evening, this car might have looked suspicious. Of course, on a hot Thursday evening in July on the northside of Indianapolis, not many people were around to notice.

A Phillips 66 gas station sat on the prime real estate on the corner of 38th Street and Meadows Drive, all too convenient for the residents in the area. It was a typical 50's station. Six pumps evenly spaced in the front parking lot, a flat-roofed building with an overhang that extended a few feet beyond the front door and windows. In a day when gas stations were really service stations, the glass and aluminum framework of the two service bays reflected the yellowish color of the streetlights on 38th Street. The Meadows Shopping Mall was just across Meadows Drive to the west, really just the entrance to the shopping center, and the Meadowbrook Apartments were wrapped around the station to the east and north. The station was closed for the evening, the white-shirted, bow-tied attendants of a day still committed to washing windshields and checking oil having gone home hours before. The quiet darkness was interrupted only by the occasional car passing on 38th Street, a major thoroughfare in the growing city. The stars filled the clear night sky and the moon illuminated the stand-alone gas pumps offering gasoline in both regular and ethyl for under 30 cents per gallon. A few clouds were beginning to drift into the dark sky. The heavy, moist July air filtered through open windows of the hundreds of meticulously spaced bungalows nearby.

Then, at 1 o'clock in the morning, the passenger door of the large, white Cadillac opened, then, a few seconds later, slammed shut again. The sound of shoes clicked a rapid, even staccato pace away from the Cadillac.

The Cadillac began backing from its parking spot parallel to the curb just inside the entrance to the

Meadowbrook Apartment complex. But it kept going. Instead of making a slow backwards turn, stopping and shifting into drive, the white Cadillac continued backwards, picking up speed as it went. The ever-increasing pace took it roaring from the parking lot, across the northbound lane of Meadows Drive, then through three complete backward circles in the divided roadway. The tires slammed the concrete curb outlining the six foot wide grassy median as thousands of pounds of steel jumped violently first up then down with each turn. The sound alternated between a squeal as the tires clawed at the black pavement and a hiss as the rear wheels spun throwing the soft green grass on the underside of car. As its accelerator forced a limitless supply of gasoline to its massive eight-cylinder, four hundred cubic inch engine, the front of the car was whipped uncontrollably, straining against the centrifugal force to break free. The front tires squealed a heart-stopping whine. Neighbors began waking from their deep sleep as the screaming tires disrupted the quiet Thursday night. Out of control and still picking up speed, it finally veered backward over the curb on the other side of Meadows Drive and smashed trunk-first into a metal utility pole.

That was the end of the line for the shiny new car and its sole occupant.

Air conditioning wasn't unheard of in the 1950's, some commercial buildings had it, but in residences it was definitely a luxury item. Some commercial air conditioning systems then were simply air forced over large blocks of ice. Even simple window air conditioners were the fare of the wealthy. It would be 20 years before middle class Indianapolis would consider air conditioners a necessity. That hot, July night, the windows in the area homes were left open to stir the stagnant summer night air. The sound of the Cadillac's final drive awakened close neighbors like Earl Alexander, who leapt from his bed and grabbed the clothes he had worn the day before to investigate.

Walking through the front door of his Meadows bungalow and looking east toward the accident scene, Mr. Alexander saw not only the impressive white Cadillac with surprising little damage given the violent sounds that preceded the crash, but also a blue and white car, a car he believed to be an Oldsmobile, but even he would have said it was hard to tell in the middle of the night. The Cadillac rested against the utility pole that was now leaning away from the Cadillac at about 30 degrees. The street light atop the damaged pole still lit the scene. The Oldsmobile had no apparent damage. Mr. Alexander told police later that as he approached the scene, he saw two men standing beside the damaged Cadillac. But, according to the groggy witness, before he could reach the accident scene, the two men turned, climbed into the Oldsmobile, and drove away.

Had the light pole not brought the runaway car to an abrupt halt, it likely would have continued until it came to rest against the rear corner of the Howard Johnson's restaurant located in the Meadowbrook shopping center just across Meadows Drive. It served as a 24-hour rest stop for travelers on the busy streets that bordered The Meadows. The colorful, familiar Howard Johnson's sign near 38th Street was redundant. The blue and orange construction was all the advertising a Howard Johnson's needed in the 1950s.

Inside the restaurant, 16 year-old Charles Hedrick was working his summer job as the night counterman. His manager was in the kitchen. With little else to do during the overnight shift, Charles routinely passed the time watching what little activity there was on the other side of the large, clean plate glass windows of the restaurant. Unlike Mr. Alexander, young Charles had seen most of the bizarre scene unfold. He had witnessed the white Cadillac's eerie, erratic run through the west windows of the square building and said he actually felt the concussion with the pole. He used the telephone to call the Indianapolis Police, then hurried to the scene of the accident, covering the 75 feet quickly. He might have been there quicker, but the simplicity of 911 was decades away.

He had to find the phone number for the police.

Young Charles Hedrick, unaccustomed to such excitement, too, witnessed two cars. And his account was similar to Earl Alexander's. He reported seeing the disabled Cadillac, and a blue car leaving the scene in too much of a hurry.

Alexander arrived at the scene just after Hedrick. Alexander had had to get dressed first. They said little to each other as they tried to understand what had just happened. Instead they focused their attention on the driver's door of the big white Caddy. With adrenaline coursing through their bodies and their hearts pounding against their chests, they expected the worst. And waited. It seemed like an eternity before the police got there.

As they waited, peering curiously into the disabled vehicle, they could see a middle-aged man dressed in a navy, summer business suit, slumped forward in the front seat, almost like he was asleep, his head resting on the steering wheel, eyes facing down. The impact had thrown him backwards. The recoil had caused him to fall forward. He hadn't hit the windshield.

Perhaps he will be OK, the two men thought.

The muffled sputtering of the Cadillac's engine and the artificial illumination of the streetlights gave the otherwise deathly still scene a surreal quality.

The men discussed the appropriate course of action and decided not to move him as they had both heard that moving an injured person might cause further injuries. They both wished help would arrive. They could feel their hearts beating in their chests. Helplessness became the main feeling. They wondered if their collective decision to leave him until help arrived was the right one.

Neither wanted to be responsible for the man's death or further injury.

Luckily, the police response was prompt. Patrolman Richard Anderson was the first law enforcement official on the scene. He had received a dispatch at 1:06 AM to investigate a routine traffic accident but it wouldn't be long before the officer would find out that this was anything but routine. He arrived from the west in his big black and white police cruiser, a single glass dome in the center of the roof moving the red light back and forth like a watch gear, his siren droning a lower and lower pitch as his car rolled to a stop facing southbound in the northbound lane of Meadows Drive.

As the officer climbed from his patrol car, Earl Alexander and Charles Hedrick ran up to the patrolman and briefed him on what they had seen. The other onlookers, now numbering several, excitedly blurted out what little they knew as well as the tall, lanky officer strode purposefully to the car. The large, heavy car door outlined in shiny chrome at the top of both the window frame and the butterfly window as well as on the bottom opened with ease to offer a clearer picture of the wealthy-looking driver. With the little apparent damage to the big Cadillac, the officer wasn't expecting the man to be unconscious. He wasn't as surprised at the sight of bloodstains at the man's open collar and the beltline of his white dress shirt. After all, even though most cars were equipped with lap seat belts, almost no one used them. Injuries in accidents were common. Crash-absorbing bumpers weren't a preferred safety item. Heavier, bigger cars with thicker steel were. Size meant safety.

Patrolman Anderson was shocked, however, when he saw where the blood was coming from.

The growing crowd pushed and craned to see inside the car. And they became eerily quiet.

Patrolman Anderson quickly identified two sources for the blood. Small, round holes, one in the neck, one in the stomach. Small, round holes that weren't made by an auto accident.

The young officer pulled the man back in the seat. The victim's head flopped onto the white leather headrest like a rag doll. Anderson roused the man to semi-consciousness. The driver began rolling his head left and right against the headrest, eyes closed tightly. A soft, uneven groan escaped the man's lips.

Anderson lightly touched the man's face and hands. The officer knew the cold, clammy feel. The skin had the temperature and consistency of child's modeling clay. This man was almost dead.

Radio communications were made from the patrol cars. Without portable radios, Anderson had no way of radioing otherwise. He returned to his patrol car, picked up his radio handset and alerted his desk sergeant that the accident call at 38th and Meadows Drive was really a gunshot wound. The driver was having a hard time breathing and was dazed, probably in shock, but now conscious.

Realizing that the victim may not have much time to live, Patrolman Anderson crouched in the soft, green grass next to the victim and identified himself as a police officer. "Can you tell me what happened," he asked.

The crew-cut officer strained to hear the inaudible reply. The victim repeated it. "Hospital. Get me to a hospital."

"There's an ambulance on the way," Anderson offered. "In the meanwhile, can you tell me what happened? Who shot you?"

The man in the Cadillac rolled his head slowly from side to side closing his eyes even tighter as if to shake off the pain. But he said nothing more.

This man was not the typical gunshot victim. He looked more like a movie star than a street thug. His expensive suit was matched with stylish two-tone brown and white shoes, a style more popular for golf shoes today. But back then, they were the epitome of money and style. His hair was neatly trimmed, despite the violent nature of the accident, and he was clean-shaven. The man had the look of money. He was a handsome, fit man who was concerned about his appearance. Other than a watch, he wore no jewelry.

Even today, a major crime invokes a certain protocol, including the summoning of a superior officer. This was the case in the Indianapolis Police Department in 1958, too. And while the officer was questioning the driver of the white Cadillac, his superior, Lieutenant Cecil London arrived on the scene. As the stocky, round, bespectacled lieutenant walked up behind the crouching Anderson, the patrolman stood and offered his brief assessment.

"It's a shooting. I can't get him to tell me what happened."

Anderson, more used to traffic stops and burglary calls, was glad to turn the case over to someone else.

The lieutenant approached the driver, crouched beside the open car door and repeated the requests for information about the assailant. Still, the man said nothing. Only repeated requests to go to a hospital.

With the man still in the car, the two lawmen couldn't pinpoint the damage done by the bullets, but they could tell they were losing him.

Lieutenant London sensed that time was running out. This was likely the only opportunity they would have to get information from this victim. Just in case the man didn't realize what was happening, London asked him pointedly, "Do you know you might die? You should tell me who shot you."

"I want to go to a hospital," was the only reply. His response was more clear and forceful, almost impatient, giving the lieutenant some encouragement about the man's prognosis.

The police lieutenant again assured the man that an ambulance was on the way. The lawmen looked at their watches. It was 1:11AM.

This time, the man offered no response of any kind. Instead, he let his head sink further into the leather headrest, closed his eyes, and took one last, deep breath.

The man was dead.

The two cops, Anderson and London were mystified. Why wouldn't the man identify the shooter? What was he doing here? Who was he?

They had plenty of questions and virtually no answers.

As promised, minutes later, the ambulance did, indeed, arrive. The arrival of the cavernous, white station wagon was telegraphed by another flashing red light and throaty siren's wail. "General Hospital" was inscribed on the front doors, just below a Red Cross emblem. General Hospital was the hospital for poor people in Indianapolis. But that was not a result of choice. It took all the people who couldn't afford to go anywhere else. But it was also the place one wanted to go if he had been shot. Due merely to practice, the staff at General Hospital was the very best at treating gunshot wounds, much better than at the pricey suburban hospitals.

The man would indeed be going to General Hospital. Unfortunately, it was not for treatment, but for an autopsy.

The first attendant, clad in no protective gear other than clean, crisp white pants and a half-zipped, white short-sleeved jacket covering his white T-shirt, opened his door before the ambulance had completely stopped, hopped out, approached the man, felt for a pulse, then shook his head. It was too late for them to do anything. "You'd better call the morgue wagon," he said.

The quest for answers to the ever-growing list of questions was just beginning.

Chapter 3

"Our pledge: Sound laws in...
1. *Local Affairs*
2. *National Affairs*
3. *International Affairs*
4. *Adequate Defense*

The restoration of Christian Principles in our relations with other nations."
1950's Democratic Party Brochure

1958 was a deadly time in Indianapolis. The city was averaging almost two murders a month in the first seven months of 1958 and the dead man in the Cadillac would make five that were unsolved going into August. The papers were beginning to question the safety of the city and residents began to wonder if the Indianapolis Police Department was overwhelmed by the growing city and its consequential problems.

In addition to the relative crime wave, the papers were also busy covering the upcoming election. Of course, no one saw much of a connection between the dead man in the Cadillac and the election of 1958.

The 1958 election however, would not be politics as usual. A strange struggle for power would play out in the offices and government buildings in downtown Indianapolis that would change the face of local, state and even national politics.

It would also set the stage for the biggest trial the Midwest had seen.

In 1948, the regents of Valparaiso University Law School, a small school in extreme northern Indiana and, of Indiana's four law schools, by far the smallest, saw fit to award a young man named Thomas Jefferson Faulconer, III a degree just as the Board of Trustees at another small, private school, Butler University, had chosen to do four years earlier. Until this time, the young man's academic career had been adequate, but well short of stellar.

Indeed, in one respect, the fact that Tom Faulconer made it to this point at all was surprising. He was born on July 5, 1923, still weeks away from a full-term delivery. His mother had attended a Fourth of July picnic and in a moment of questionable judgment, had taken a rather raucous car ride, automobiles still considered a novelty to many. The wild ride induced an early labor and she gave birth just after midnight. Doctors were unsure the tiny child would survive. But after spending several weeks in an incubator, he was deemed healthy enough to be removed.

The son of a railroad executive, the young boy enjoyed a typical depression-era childhood in Indianapolis, Indiana. From there, it was on to college.

Upon his graduation from Butler University in 1945 and discharge from the mandatory service in the U.S. military, he quickly realized that his history degree from the small, private school limited his future options to graduate school and teaching. Enamored with neither option, he opted for law school. He had been the first in his family to graduate from college, and now was attempting to be the first to become a lawyer.

Until the 1970's, law schools carefully controlled the admissions process. Consequently, successful completion of the law school and passage of a state bar exam was as close to a guarantee of success as one could get. Competition for jobs in law firms was miniscule by today's standards. The reason was simple supply and demand. There were just not that many lawyers. Plus, the public held them in high esteem.

The majority of lawyers in the 1950's were in practice for themselves or, possibly, in a partnership or office sharing arrangement with one or two others. Big, national, or even regional law firms were as unthinkable in those days as attorneys advertising on television. Clients hired lawyers, not law firms. Personal relationships and competency were paramount.

New lawyers weren't looking for jobs. They were settling into careers.

However, new lawyers, Tom included, learned quite quickly, that law school had not necessarily taught them to practice law properly. A law school's main objective is to teach men and women to think like lawyers using legal reasoning and to find the rules of law when needed. The public didn't understand that then and still doesn't now. And lawyers are too proud to tell otherwise.

Tom Faulconer felt he knew dangerously little when he emerged from Valparaiso Law School in 1948.

His feeling was right.

So, again, faced with another of life's crossroads, the young man opted for the route from law school that many lawyers took at such a stage in their early careers. He applied for, was offered and accepted a job with the Buckeye Union Insurance Company back in his hometown of Indianapolis as a claims adjuster. Until the 1960's, most insurance companies preferred, or even required their claims adjusters to be attorneys. The insurance companies needed someone who could read and interpret a contract, so who better than someone with a legal background to get the job done?

The position would give the young man needed experience, income, and a chance to take the bar exam.

Most new employees approach their first days with great anticipation and, albeit unspoken, visions of greatness in their new opportunity. But Tom knew that this new job wasn't what he wanted to do in the long term. He hadn't spent the toughest years of his life in law school to work for someone else. He hadn't struggled to prepare himself for and to pass the Indiana Bar Exam to work a job in an insurance company. He wanted his own law practice. More precisely, he wanted more than anything to be a judge. But he had to be a lawyer first.

By April, 1950, Tom had saved up some money and, against the better advice of his family and friends, he quit his $250 a month job, turned in his company car and rented an office in a downtown building for the princely sum of $100 per month. His father was certain he was nuts, but kept his fatherly advice to himself.

Tom didn't know any other lawyers in town to speak of, and didn't have a single client. Yet on April 1, 1950, the Law Office of Thomas J. Faulconer was open for business. Coincidentally, it was April Fool's Day, irony not lost on the new lawyer. Thankfully, few others would make the connection.

Anticipation gave way to concern as, predictably, prospective clients failed to knock down the door to hire the young, inexperienced lawyer. Most months he made just enough to pay his rent.

Some months, he made enough to eat, too.

His new adventure gave him another benefit, one that the adjuster's job at Buckeye Union had not afforded. It may have been one that he would have readily traded for a greater income and more legal work, but in this early stage of his career, he had no such choice.

Tom found he had an abundance of free time.

Consequently, he found another pursuit that, while it didn't contribute to his income in 1950, would serve him well later. He became involved in the Democratic Party in Indiana. With his admittedly abundant lack of commitments, he dove into local and state politics headfirst. Politics, even on the local level, suited him well.

Soon, he had been elected to the position of precinct committeeman in the neighborhood in which he lived.

Life in politics did provide him some new clients, but most of all, it provided him with contacts. These contacts would prove the basis for much of his career.

Despite his enjoyment of the political process, he was constantly and consistently reminded that politics didn't necessarily put food on his table. Confidentially the young man was getting somewhat discouraged by this point, so he began seeking the advice of some of the other lawyers he had met by now, most of them through his work with the Democrats.

The advice he got was plentiful and rang a familiar tone. To make it, they told him, he needed to get a part-time job. The income would allow him to pay his bills while he would still have time to develop his practice. Eventually, the practice would squeeze out the part-time job. It all sounded simple and made complete sense. So he immediately set out to find a part-time job.

Friends also recommended he contact the prosecutor's office in Marion County, where Indianapolis is located. After all, the prosecutor was a Democrat. With his work for the party, surely he could get a part-time job there, they said.

Infused with new confidence and optimism, Tom orchestrated a masterful campaign. He wrote, called and visited the prosecutor's office in Marion County on a regular basis. He extolled his loyalty to the Democrat Party at every opportunity. He searched for contacts that could serve as third party influences for him. He even had his girlfriend contact people she knew there. He followed up regularly with every one of his limited contacts. Little else could have been done.

But he got no response. Not even an interview. In fact, not even a rejection letter. No one at the prosecutor's office would give him the time of day.

And, even though he did try to find other opportunities, he didn't have any better luck anywhere else, either.

By this time fully, and deservedly, discouraged, Tom Faulconer, attorney at law, wondered if his family had been right. The $250 a month check from Buckeye Union's bank account plus a car was looking very good at this point. But crawling back would be an admission of failure. And he wasn't quite ready for that—yet. Others had done this successfully. Surely, he could, too.

Luckily, as he would many times during his life, he found that fate was on his side. What happened next started a series of events in his life that could only be described as being in the right place at the right time.

One spring day, just a few months after he had opened his office, he was walking on Market Street, the busy downtown thoroughfare that intersects Monument Circle in the center of town and is home to city landmarks such as the City Market where locals hawk their produce and other goods. A dentist in town named Thomas Scanlon, who Faulconer knew from his involvement in the Democratic Party, met him from the other direction. The two men began to talk. Predictably, Scanlon asked him how things were going. Tom tried to put his best face forward, but had to reluctantly admit that things could be better.

Over the next several minutes, he told of his numerous setbacks in trying to find a part-time job to help pay the bills.

Scanlon listened courteously, then blurted, "You are in luck, my friend."

Before Tom knew what was happening, Scanlon had hold of his coat and together they walked to see a friend of Scanlon's who was rumored to have a part-time job available.

Not five minutes later, the two were in the office of Philip Bayt, Controller for the City of Indianapolis.

The job of City Controller in 1950 was a position of power, although very few recognized it. Indeed, the rare Indianapolis resident would have even been able to identify the controller. But, while to many, controller may not have seemed to be much of a position in city government, the truth was that it was about as powerful as you could get in those days. After all, the controller in Indianapolis had all of the purse strings. The controller was the embodiment of the famous paraphrase of the golden rule: Whoever has the gold makes the rules.

In the city government in 1950, Phil Bayt also had another source of power. With the exception of a few high level, high visibility positions, he also made most of the public appointments. Technically and legally, the mayor made the appointments. But in virtually every case, he deferred to the controller and put his rubber stamp on the paperwork.

It seemed that the controller was second in command, a "vice mayor" of sorts. In fact, legally, the same was true. In the event of the death of the mayor, by law the controller would take over.

In a matter of moments, the young lawyer's luck had seemingly changed for the better.

And in a matter of moments, it would change back.

Unfortunately, the first news that Mr. Bayt had was not good. Indeed, the City of Indianapolis was looking for an attorney to represent the Sanitation Department. But, he informed Scanlon, with the anxious young lawyer listening, he had already filled the part-time position. Someone else was to be named shortly.

However, for whatever reason, the City Controller took a shine to the new lawyer. During the course of the conversation that day, Bayt asked him where he had his office and what kind of work he was doing. Soon, Bayt told him that he had a spare office in his own law firm and if the new lawyer would come to work with him, taking his overflow of cases while still developing his own practice, Bayt would pay all his expenses.

It was an offer that clearly surprised the recipient.

So many things were different in 1950. Even being the City Controller in Indianapolis in 1950 was much different than it is today. Certainly, Indianapolis was a large city by any standards, but the fact is, it pretty much governed itself. Not much changed in this city that would, in a few years, earn the nickname, "Naptown." It was in the midst of an urban expansion and many residents were opting to move further and further away from downtown, but virtually all of the businesses were still located within the mile square that comprised downtown Indianapolis. The city was looking more and more like a doughnut. People lived in the outer ring, but worked in the middle. As a result, during the workday, downtown Indianapolis evoked a very distinct small-town feel.

And while the controller's job was, technically, a full-time position, it didn't take forty hours a week to do the job. So Bayt also maintained his previous occupation at the same time. Phil Bayt's law practice stayed open for business.

Tom was enthused after the meeting but hesitated and the days following the conversation with Bayt turned to a week. He did nothing to pursue the opportunity. Perhaps he felt as though the offer was simply made out of politeness or maybe as a favor to Bayt's friend, Dr. Scanlon. Perhaps he simply thought it was too good to be true. In any case, Bayt got tired of waiting. Days later, Tom was quite surprised when Phil Bayt called him to follow up on his offer.

"What have you decided about my office?" Bayt demanded.

Truthfully, he hadn't decided anything. He hadn't really even thought about it.

Removing his round, wire-rimmed glasses and running his hand through his slightly thinning reddish-blonde hair, he responded, "Well, I just haven't made up my mind yet."

"Could I think about it for a few more days?" he asked doing his best to think on his feet.

This should have been an easy decision for any young lawyer, especially one in need of a pipeline for new clients. But deep down, reflecting on his recent difficulties in making ends meet, Tom was a pessimist at this point. What did Bayt want from him, he wondered. Was there anything in this arrangement that could harm him or his fragile, embryonic reputation? Getting in the wrong political circles could cost him his shot at a judgeship later. He had to tread carefully.

The truth was, Bayt was an unknown quantity. Tom knew he had to proceed cautiously. One wrong move and his promising career could be tarnished forever, he reasoned.

So he set out to investigate Mr. Philip Bayt. Methodically, he began phoning the few friends he had developed who were attorneys in Indianapolis and contacting his friends in politics. The response was consistent. Phil Bayt was the best thing that could happen to this young man's career, they said.

They were right.

In September of 1950, the decision made, he moved from his office of six months. He moved in with Phil Bayt.

The two got along well. Bayt was preoccupied with his position as controller and Tom finally had some breathing room in his previously tight finances. But he had barely finished unpacking when his world would change again.

Not even two months later, on November 15, 1950, the then-current Mayor of Indianapolis, Al Feeney, on his 58th birthday, died unexpectedly. Hours later, the city controller was taking the oath as Mayor of Indianapolis.

Literally within days Tom had gone from a new lawyer with few contacts and even fewer clients to an associate in the law office of the mayor.

Television was a novelty back in 1950, in fact, Indianapolis only had one station on the air and it only broadcast a few evenings a week. The rest of the time, was either snow or the black and white test pattern that looked like a target for a shooting range. Still, the novelty of wireless pictures continued to capture the fancy of many. They would stand in front of appliance store windows watching anything that was on—including the test pattern. Radio was still primarily for entertainment, so that meant the several newspapers in the city were the main sources for news.

By the time notices of Tom's new law office location were printed by the newspapers, Bayt had already become mayor. So, instead of announcing his association with the city controller, a fact that would elicit little excitement, the newspapers carried articles announcing the new lawyer in the mayor's office.

Suddenly, Faulconer was well known.

And in a testament to the lesson that it is more who you know than what you know, one of the first phone calls Faulconer received after the articles appeared in the papers was from the Marion County Prosecutor. Surprisingly, he did, indeed, have a part-time position for a young, rising star in the Democratic party. Days later, the young, inexperienced lawyer was appointed, not a deputy prosecutor, the typical position for a new lawyer, but Chief Deputy Prosecutor in the Marion County Juvenile Court.

Other lawyers began sending letters of congratulations.

How quickly fortunes could change.

The office of mayor was not unlike the office of controller in that, while technically a full-time position, it could be done in substantially less time. Bayt, like the mayors before him, decided to also maintain his dual careers by continuing his law practice in addition to performing his obligations as mayor. Of course, the increased exposure and increased responsibilities meant he had less time to devote to his practice. Tom became the beneficiary of this fact, inheriting several clients from the new mayor.

Tom's relationship with the mayor provided the fuel needed to launch his career.

But, once again, it looked as though he would run out of gas all too soon.

Bayt's mayoral term was only one year. The former Mayor Feeney's term expired in 1951 and so Phil Bayt would be forced to defend his position as mayor, first in a primary, then in the general election.

The primary was uneventful. Although the Democrats did present a few other candidates for mayor, they presented little challenge to the already powerful incumbent.

Phil Bayt was the man for the Democratic Party in 1951.

In the short retrospective since leaving Buckeye Union, Tom had quickly come to appreciate the causation of his few, but major successes thus far. Virtually everything that had happened to him, everyone he met and many of the clients he secured were traceable directly to his work in the Democratic Party and Phil Bayt. Understandably, he vowed to continue to support them both.

Consequently, in 1951, he worked tirelessly for the campaign of Phil Bayt. And Bayt's prospects looked exceedingly good. Tom would attend dinners, picnics, going just about anywhere he could to stump for his new mentor, Phil Bayt.

Bolstered by his recent good fortune and confident of his work on a campaign in which he believed strongly, Faulconer worked tirelessly on behalf of Mayor Bayt's reelection campaign.

And on the night of the general election in November of 1951, he felt so strongly about his candidate's chances, the newlywed of 11 months came home to his wife and boldly predicted victory for Phil Bayt. There was no way he could lose!

Ironically, at that very moment, Bayt was at Democratic headquarters conceding the race to his opponent, Judge Alex Clark, the Republican candidate.

Phil Bayt, Tom's main supporter, both emotionally and financially, had lost the election.

In a sense, so had Tom Faulconer.

But the roller coaster ride of emotions was not over yet. Soon after his loss, Bayt was appointed the judge in Municipal Court #3 in Marion County. The judge's job in Municipal Court #3 was an appointed position. However, by law, if the current judge was unable to carry out his term, through death, illness, conviction of a crime or resignation, a new judge would be appointed to complete the term.

Luckily for both Bayt and Faulconer, where one door closed, another opened for the ousted mayor. The judge in Municipal Court #3 abruptly quit to become an assistant to the National Democrat Party Chairman.

Phil Bayt was quickly appointed to become the judge of that court.

And so, once again, Phil Bayt took care of the young lawyer.

More often than the public realizes, sitting judges are disqualified to hear cases due to conflicts of interest, or are simply unable to participate due to vacations and other obligations. Whenever possible, Bayt appointed the young man as pro tem, or temporary judge, to hear those cases when Judge Bayt couldn't be in court.

The pro tem positions were another boon for Tom's career. They provided him with the opportunity to see what it was like to be a judge. After all, this was his ultimate career goal. This temporary arrangement allowed him to experience it without making the long-term commitment to the job.

Frankly, he liked it.

The appointments also got his name in front of the public again. The newspapers reported virtually every decision and action of every judge in the county. This included Judge Pro Tem Tom Faulconer. The frequent publicity served him well.

By 1952, he was on his way to becoming a household name, at least in Indianapolis, Indiana.

On the surface, the election in 1951 had looked much like any other. But in truth, the election of 1951 masked the simmering emotions of the Democrat Party in Indianapolis. The party had a split in ideology and leadership that was becoming quite raw, if not yet very public.

The National Chairman of the Democratic Party at the time was from Indiana. He was a successful family banker named Frank McKinney. The McKinneys owned and controlled one of the largest banks in Indiana and Frank had parlayed that wealth and power into a formidable political career. And even though McKinney was hundreds of miles away in Washington, D.C., he still ruled the party in Indiana and, until now, no one dared question his authority.

Phil Bayt and a small group of others in Indiana decided they didn't much care for this arrangement. To tell the truth, they didn't care for Frank McKinney either. So Phil Bayt began working on a plan to take control of the party. And he asked his young lawyer friend, among others, to help.

The ingenious Bayt devised a plan to unseat the leaders of the Democrat Party in Indiana. The foothold on the party by the McKinney supporters was solid. If Bayt were to succeed, he would not be able to do so by going toe-to-toe in elections. That had been tried and didn't work. The McKinney side had the power, the offices and the money.

But Bayt had the plan.

Bayt and his cohorts began having clandestine meetings designed to plot the future of the party. In a rather brilliant move, Bayt recruited "unofficial" ward chairmen who would contact the precinct committeemen in the individual neighborhoods and attempt to sway their support to Bayt's Democrats and away from McKinney.

For the coming election, the Democratic Party had two parallel systems, each with its own ward chairmen and political bosses.

Obviously, these mostly young, idealistic and unofficial ward chairmen had none of the power the officially appointed McKinney ward chairmen had. But they had every bit as much enthusiasm. Plus, most of them also held positions in the "legitimate" party, as true ward chairmen and precinct committeemen, thus they also had an air of legitimacy when talking to the precincts.

Their takeover plan would be tested in the election of 1954.

After just a few years of sharing office space in Phil Bayt's office, Tom's invaluable experience had only served to reinforce his belief that he wanted to be a judge. His notoriety and his continued work in the Democratic Party combined to make him a viable candidate in the election in 1954. At the time, there were two criminal courts in Marion County and he set his sights on what he saw as the best one, Criminal Court #1.

Criminal Court #1 was the original court in Marion County devoted exclusively to felony criminal cases. The courtroom was huge, with a high ceiling, ornate woodwork and a judge's bench that sat five feet above everyone else in the room. Expensive wood permeated the room and created muted echoes that caused reverential feelings in anyone and everyone who entered. A balcony lined one wall and crown moldings fully two feet thick capped all four walls where they met the ceiling. Heavy wooden chairs comprised the gallery, separated from the dispensation of justice by dark wood balustrades. It was a most impressive courtroom. The judge's chambers were impressive and roomy.

No question, Criminal Court #1 was the one he wanted.

This was his shot. With the backing of Phil Bayt and the optimism and enthusiasm of the Bayt machine, Tom threw himself wholeheartedly into the race with the reckless abandon of his youth. Every ounce of energy went toward getting elected.

Unfortunately, some of that energy should have been directed at maintaining his fledgling law practice. He intentionally never let it enter into his mind that he would lose. He could have taught Dale Carnegie lessons in positive thinking. And since he wouldn't need his law practice after the victory, he just sort of let it go.

That was a lesson he would remember for the rest of his life.

Winning Criminal Court #1 would actually take two wins. First, he had to fight his way through the May primary. Then, assuming he survived the primary, and he was certain he would, he would have to face a Republican opponent in the general election in November.

Only one other candidate filed for the Democrat nomination for Criminal Court #1. Gordon Davis was a young lawyer as well at the time, but, having not received some of the good luck and publicity that Tom had enjoyed, was at a significant disadvantage. The fact is that many attorneys mounted token campaigns in the primaries simply to get some free publicity in hopes of jump-starting their practice.

Whatever his reason for running, Gordon Davis didn't put up much of a fight.

In addition, the Democrat Party's recommended slate of candidates that was developed at the party's convention of precinct committeemen and women just before the primary recommended Faulconer over Davis.

Political "machines" were all the rage in the 1950's. Huey Long had his in Louisiana and Chicago had the Daleys. Former President Truman credited his entry into politics to a political machine. Even in Indiana, the election in 1954 gave undeniable proof of the power of a political boss, even one under a serious challenge. The unofficial Democrat ward chairmen were making plenty of trouble for McKinney and his clan. The old-line Democrats were beginning to feel the heat. But party boss McKinney still had a ward chairman loyal to him in the 12th ward. The ward chairman, Joe Howard, didn't like the Bayt Democrats and wasn't about to let one of them win in his ward.

When the primary votes were tallied, Tom had won every ward in Marion County but one.

He didn't get a *single* vote in Joe Howard's ward. Not one.

But when the laborious process of counting all of the primary votes was completed, Tom Faulconer had defeated Gordon Davis easily.

Tom would be the Democratic Party's choice for Judge in Marion County Criminal Court #1 in November of 1954.

To the surprise of no one, the general election proved to be much tougher. And again, more so, if possible, every ounce of energy and enthusiasm was poured into the campaign.

Tom had already learned that in politics judges' positions usually went the way of the party. In other words, if the Democrats won, he would likely win. If the Democrats lost, he would likely lose. Very few voters knew enough about the individual candidates in the "lesser" races. They traditionally voted party lines more so on these races than on the "marquee" races. But he still did all he could to increase his chances in the race.

November came quickly. Tom had spent the summer traveling to family reunions, precinct meetings, block parties and anywhere else he could shake hands and maybe influence a few voters. The frequent dinners of fried chicken, biscuits and brownies over the months of campaigning eventually took its toll on his youthful physique. By his early thirties, his 5' 10" frame was enveloped by over 200 pounds.

Now the moment of truth was arriving and soon he would see if his work had paid off.

In November of 1954, the votes were cast in the general election. The counting began immediately upon the polls closing at 6:00 PM.

When the final tally was announced by the election board, Tom learned he would not occupy the bench in Criminal Court #1. He had lost.

The Republicans had won in a proverbial landslide. In fact, of all the county offices up for grabs, only one went to a Democrat. Robert O'Neal would be sheriff.

The Democrats had been slaughtered. And Tom Faulconer had, too, 107,000 votes to 88,000.

But in a strange sense, even though he wasn't running for an elected office in 1954, Democrat Phil Bayt had won.

Bayt's clandestine sabotage of the McKinney machine had caused just the split in the party that he and the others had hoped for. The rift that Bayt's group caused in the Indiana Democratic Party succeeded in toppling the state chairman of the party. McKinney had lost his power base in Indiana. Soon, the rest of the country had taken notice of McKinney's difficulties in his home state of Indiana.

By early 1955, McKinney's career as National Party Chairman was over.

In seven, very short years, Tom had quit his job, opened, then moved his law office, run for public office, was an associate of the mayor of a large city, married, had two daughters and helped change the face of national politics.

And celebrated his 32nd birthday.

The moral victories within the party were of little consolation, though. Once again, the loss was personally devastating. He had neglected his law practice to the point that there was little to return to. The feelings of devastation turned to apathy. Weeks of doing nothing turned to a month. The young lawyer took the public rejection personally.

He vowed never to assume victory again.

Eventually, Tom did pull himself up and return to his law practice. But the bitter taste of his defeat was never far from his mind.

The policemen began searching the dead man's clothing and found his wallet, neat, intact and loaded with $210, an enviable sum for that day - the equivalent of over $1,200 today! $210 was certainly a sum worthy of a robbery attempt. Yet, there was absolutely no evidence of robbery. Strangely, it was untouched.

Their further search of the car revealed little else of significance besides a glimpse into the leisurely life of the owner. The trunk contained a box of golf balls, a student pilot's manual, two life jackets and a case of expensive scotch. The backseat held two diving masks and a snorkel. He apparently had an enviable lifestyle, engaging in leisurely pursuits that required a significant income. The policemen didn't find any usable fingerprints.

Robbery certainly didn't look like the motive.

The wallet also contained cards identifying the owner as Forrest Teel. Mr. Teel's address was shown as Washington Boulevard, an area on the northside of the city, home to some of its most rich and powerful.

As the crowd grew larger, a local resident, obviously hurriedly dressed to satisfy his natural curiosity, stepped forward. "I know who he is," he said to the policemen.

"Who?" Lieutenant London quickly turned and asked.

"He's one of the big bosses out at the drug company—one of the *big* bosses, in the front office. His name's Teel—Forrest Teel."

Forrest Teel, one of Indianapolis' most important, most prominent citizens was dead.

Chapter 4

"Police Hunt Two Cars In Slaying Of Lilly Executive—Victim's Last Word Provides No Clue."
Page 1 Headline, Indianapolis News
July 31, 1958

The "Drug Company" needed no further explanation to someone who lived in Indiana. Indianapolis was home to but one business of significant size during much of the twentieth century and the locals embraced their "drug company."

Eli Lilly and Company was the quintessential Horatio Alger story. It was started in 1876 by 38 year-old pharmaceutical chemist Colonel Eli Lilly. The colonel was a veteran of the Civil War that had ended a decade earlier. Frustrated by the lack of effectiveness, consistency and quality in pharmaceutical preparations, he laid out his plan to offer pharmaceuticals of the highest quality possible. At its inception, Eli Lilly and Company offered many of the "cures" of the day, including tonics and elixirs and "cure-alls" in fancy brown bottles with raised writing. It wasn't until a few years later, after adding a full-time chemist, and improving on many of the techniques of the day, his small company would begin an incredible phase of growth that would last literally for generations. Today, Lilly's best-known product is the antidepressant drug Prozac. However, while Prozac is Lilly's dance partner today, it is not the date that brought it to the dance.

In the early 1920s, a chemist, George Henry Alexander Clowes, attended a lecture on the promise of insulin in the treatment of diabetes. Until this time diabetes was controlled by a very strict diet, which accurately earned the name, the "Starvation Diet." Those unfortunate souls that contracted the disease were lucky to live another two years on the difficult food plan.

But the alternative was even less promising.

More than anyone else in the lecture, Clowes was taken by the promise of insulin. In incredibly small doses, it was amazingly effective. He set about testing and analyzing data and samples as soon as he returned to his lab. Others at the lecture failed, for whatever reason, to see the promise in the drug that Clowes did.

The result of his hard work and foresight was a one year headstart on other pharmaceutical companies for the introduction of insulin to market.

That was an advantage from which it would take almost one hundred years for the rest of the industry to recover.

The company would thrive with the Colonel at the helm. And it would continue to thrive as his son, Josiah K. Lilly, Sr., and two of his grandsons, Eli Lilly and Josiah K. Lilly, Jr., each took turns at the reins.

In the ensuing decades, Lilly was fortunate enough to develop several groundbreaking antibiotics which further fueled the growth of the company.

The Lilly family ran the company until 1953. For the first time, a non-Lilly family president was named. However, Josiah. K. Lilly, Jr, or J.K., remained as chairman and honorary chairman.

Still, as late as 1958, Lilly, and Indianapolis, was continuing to adjust to life without the Lilly family at the helm.

Over the almost 100 years of Lilly's existence, the company's and the family's generosity had been unmatched. The Lilly name graced everything from college libraries to pavilions. Even the family of chemist Clowes would share its good fortune with the city, donating the money for the acoustically "perfect" Clowes Hall on the campus of Butler University—just a few hundred yards from the Lilly Library.

In the end, both the company and the city survived quite well.

The southside of downtown Indianapolis, just south of the warehouse district where truck drivers and steelworkers came to buy cigars fresh off the railcars, became Lilly's neighborhood. The growing company frequently acquired land and buildings to house the equipment and personnel needed to sustain its incredible growth. The result was, and is, a disjointed, mismatched group of buildings, for the most part, all within walking distance of each other.

The company was and is the pride of Indianapolis. A job at Lilly was a coveted prize. And those that rose to its highest ranks were rewarded with perks of which Indianapolis' ordinary citizens could only dream, including exorbitant salaries, Cadillacs and private dining rooms and washrooms.

Forrest Teel had achieved just that level of success. By the fateful summer of 1958, he was the Executive Vice President of Marketing and President of the company's successful and increasingly important international division. He was the number two man at the most powerful pharmaceutical company in the world.

Teel had it all. He belonged to the right country club. He lived in a house on Washington Boulevard with a value estimated at over $50,000. Today, those same Washington Boulevard addresses command hundreds of thousands of dollars, and still attract the well-to-do of Indianapolis.

He was athletic, charming, handsome, rich and powerful. People recognized him and, apparently, liked him.

He was directly responsible for the careers of several Lilly employees. Put simply, if he liked you, you were in. Forrest Teel was the corporate version of a Hollywood star maker. Years later, employees at Lilly would tell of lackluster careers jumpstarted by chance meetings with the handsome executive, many taking place over meals or golf at the country club, or as a result of conversation about flying, his latest passion.

He had recently been named to the board of directors of the pharmaceutical giant.

By 1958, the Eli Lilly Company was the largest pharmaceutical concern in the world. And Forrest Teel was a big fish in a big pond.

Teel was one of those people to whom life seemed to come entirely too easy. He was well known in his community and had the admiration of literally thousands of Lilly employees worldwide. He spoke three languages, all of them fluently. He had the time and means to pursue virtually any interest he desired. He learned to scuba dive, traveled extensively in an era in which long distance travel was the exception, and he was developing his burgeoning passion for aircraft.

Some speculated that he would someday become president of the entire corporation. They may well have been right.

In the 50's, the Country Club of Indianapolis was one of the premier cultural societies in central Indiana. The dues were pricey, certainly out of reach of blue-collar workers and, for many professionals, a stretch as well.

But Teel was not simply a member, he was on the board of directors making decisions from design, remodel and expansion of the club's facilities, to new member invitations. He was a staple on the club golf course and regularly turned in enviable scores. Many of his employees began playing the game in hopes of impressing, or at least interesting the boss.

Golf may have been a pastime for the wealthy, but flying was clearly a sport of kings in the 50's. Most of the population had never been on an airliner or airplane. Commercial aviation was, at best, in its infancy. National Airlines had introduced the country's first regularly scheduled domestic flights within the last year. Even fewer were lucky enough to fly in a private airplane.

But by 1958, Forrest Teel had not only begun private flying lessons, he was doing so in his own airplane. He had rented a hangar at the nearby Sky Harbor airport and kept it inside, another luxury enjoyed by precious few.

Forrest Teel was a true man of the world.

Unfortunately, according to many, he knew it. The rules applied to others, not to Mr. Teel. To many, he was charming. To others, he was pompous. To still others, he was unbearable. He had the power, the money, the friends and prestige to overcome any difficulties, to pry himself from any jam.

Except one.

And the death of Forrest Teel would send shock waves through the corporate halls of Eli Lilly and Company.

Early speculation was that Teel had been to the airport that night for a class and stopped at one of the restaurants in the Meadows area for dinner on his way home. But this theory was quickly discarded since the airport didn't hold classes at night and no one in any of the nearby restaurants remembered seeing Mr. Teel.

Investigators would later learn that he had called his house earlier in the evening to say he was going to the country club for his board meeting that night and wouldn't be home until late.

But the country club reported he had called to say he couldn't make the meeting. He reportedly did so often.

In spite of a diligent search, no one knew what he was doing in The Meadows in the middle of a Thursday night.

As occurs in murder cases, other law enforcement personnel began arriving at the scene in the minutes that followed. Sergeants Phillip Sanders and Gene Smith, both of the homicide division, innocently thought they had arrived at the scene of a "routine" murder, whatever that was. Lt. London quickly told them that this was going to be anything but "run of the mill." The lawmen began formulating possible scenarios.

Captain Michael Smiley, the number two man in the homicide division arrived at the scene not long after the pieces of this puzzle began to come together. He was approached by the two Detective Sergeants who had preceded him and he officially joined the investigation.

By the time Capt. Smiley arrived, Sergeants Sanders and Smith had begun to interview the witnesses and formulate theories. They briefed their captain soon after. Among their findings was a small, flat lead bullet smaller than a dime, found inside the car, beside the seat where the victim lay, head back, the empty stare of death in his open eyes, his slack jaw open slightly. His dark blue suit coat lay draped over the left side of the bottom of the driver's seat, cascading out the open door.

The men couldn't locate any exit wounds on the body that would explain the slug on the floorboard. Apparently, the killer missed at least once, they surmised.

In addition to the stray bullet, Sanders, a large man with short, dark hair and built like a football player, offered his opinion that the victim had, in reality, been shot three times, not two - once in the neck, once in the side and once in the hip. All of these wounds were on his right side, the passenger side of the car. Sanders also guessed that, due to the size of the bullet holes, this crime was committed with a twenty-two or maybe a twenty-five-caliber gun. Knowing that a professional would never use such a small gun, the three men ruled out any kind of a "hit."

The possibility of suicide was quickly dismissed as well. The pattern of the bullet wounds would be extremely difficult for one to self-inflict, the chances of a miss were unlikely and suicides wouldn't typically shoot themselves in the neck, stomach and hip. A head or chest shot would have been much more effective and efficient. And why would he kill himself, anyway?

Besides, most importantly, there was no gun.

The men joked that a gun of that caliber was more like a "woman's gun." It was humor only a homicide detective would appreciate.

The detectives began to examine the body more closely. They easily identified powder burns indicating that Mr. Teel was shot at close range. They unbuttoned his coat and stripped away his jacket. They unbuckled his belt and unzipped his pants slightly, looking for more wounds. They found none.

Great police detectives say that two of the traits that make a good detective are his passion and his ability to attempt to formulate theories that fit the evidence. While it may seem unbelievably simple to a layperson, in practice, it is actually quite difficult not to come to an early conclusion and then find the evidence to support the conclusion.

Even the veteran homicide detectives must check themselves periodically to assure that they are not falling into this common trap. If the detectives had begun the investigation with the thought of suicide in mind, they may well have subconsciously ignored evidence that might disprove this theory. Many investigations have been "solved" in the minds of the investigating detectives only to have it unravel within the walls of a courtroom when the defense attorneys take a more "objective" and critical view.

It doesn't take long before a detective learns that criminal investigations are as much about figuring out what didn't happen as they are about finding out what did.

The veteran detectives began to theorize based on what they had so far.

Other witnesses began gathering as the early morning hours progressed. The hot summer sun would be rising soon. Each witness was methodically and thoroughly interviewed and documented. The stories were remarkably similar. Some had simply heard tires squealing. Others had seen the two mysterious men who left the scene doing so in a cream-colored Cadillac rather than the blue and white Oldsmobile. Still others reported the blue and white car leaving in a hurry.

And several reported hearing what they thought were firecrackers just before the incident.

But they were not hearing mischievous teens celebrating a late Fourth of July. They were hearing a murder that would soon captivate the world.

Soon, the deputy coroner arrived and made the official pronouncement of the death of Forrest Teel. Soon after, the detectives watched closely as morgue attendants lifted the body from the car, careful not to destroy evidence. Police photographers snapped shots as the body was lain on the stretcher, its shirt and coat falling open to reveal the small but fatal bullet holes. Three men slid it into the gaping door of the waiting black hearse station wagon.

It seemed for some reason, someone wanted Mr. Teel dead.

In spite of what women's magazines say today, even in the best of social and economic times, which the 1950's seemed to be, life is not necessarily easy for a divorced woman trying to make it in a decidedly man's world. But forty-something Connie Conrad Keifer Nicholas was determined that she was going to make it. Her life of struggle could have made an interesting story in itself.

The odds were stacked against Connie from the beginning.

By her own admission, born in Lexington, Kentucky in 1914, Minnie Bell Conrad, or "Connie" as she would come to be called, was uprooted when she was but three years old when her family moved to Portsmouth, Oregon. Her father, Charles, opened a restaurant in Portsmouth and, like any small businessperson in the early years of a venture, struggled too long and too hard to make the restaurant successful. To help with the long hours required in the restaurant business, Connie's mom, Emma, would eventually be drawn into the vacuum the business created.

Of course, the family chipped in to help when possible at the restaurant. Connie would later say that one of her first memories was standing on a soapbox in the kitchen of the restaurant washing dirty dishes. She was about six years old.

Both parents knew that they were, in a sense, neglecting their four children. The hard work that needed to be done would deprive the Conrad children of the carefree childhood the other children in town had. But they also knew that if they could just turn the corner, it would all pay off, for them and their family.

Thankfully, by the early 1920's, the hard work had begun to do just that. The restaurant had become a staple of Portsmouth social life and was finally turning a steady profit. Of course, like so many other businesspeople, the Conrads didn't relax their obligations. They continued to toil long hours at the restaurant.

In 1923, however, things would change drastically and suddenly for the Conrads.

In 1923, Connie turned 9 years old. That same year, her father died unexpectedly. The dynamics of the Conrad family had changed in an instant. Her mother was now a single parent to four children left alone to nurture the business that was their only source of income. She faced an uncertain future in a time when government support for struggling parents was not an option. As Connie's mom saw it, she had but one option. She had to continue to run the restaurant, their sole source of income.

Surely, Connie's mom did her best to keep the restaurant going. But her heart was not in it. She felt the guilt of neglecting her family duties at the same time she was forced to devote so much of her time and energy to the restaurant.

In the end, she just couldn't do it.

The Conrads struggled to hold the family together for two more years. Mrs. Conrad continued her long hours and the children pitched in at the expense of developing friendships, social skills and long-term relationships so important at that age.

By 1925, the family was in disarray. Connie's mom was in a sanitarium, the restaurant was closed and Connie, her younger sister, Mabel, and her two older brothers, Hugh and Russell, were split among various relatives.

This early part of Connie's life would plant the seeds for her lifelong search for true love and devotion, the two most important things in her life that she never had as a child.

However, even this life of struggle would get worse.

Connie, two years later at the tender age of 11, would be dealt yet another devastating blow. Her mother contracted tuberculosis and died.

That same year, Connie moved back to Kentucky to live with her uncle, W.R. Conrad in the town of Shelbyville. By that time, her older brothers were old enough to support themselves. Her uncle felt two children would be too much of a burden on him and his family, so Mabel was left with others.

In the short, tragic life of an 11 year-old, Connie Conrad had suffered more than most people suffer in a lifetime.

She would be shuffled several more times. After being sent to live with an aunt, the aunt then moved to Zionsville, Indiana. Another move to Indianapolis, and Connie began her high school career at Shortridge High School on the northside of Indianapolis.

By the ninth grade, she was virtually on her own.

But the determined young girl persevered, supporting herself with odd jobs. Most often, she worked as a housekeeper in return for room and board. But even at that young age, she understood the value of a high school diploma.

Amazingly, against all odds, at the age of 20, Connie graduated from Shortridge High School.

Her childhood was officially over. In reality, it had ended years before.

She probably never knew it consciously, but the feelings of loss and rejection were forever imprinted on Connie's personality. They would cloud her judgment and color her life forever. Her turbulent childhood had taught her much about survival. She learned what was important, and how to get it. She learned how to make people like her. She could be charming and engaging—when she wanted to. She could be tempestuous as well.

After graduation, Connie entered the work force full time. She spent a short time working at Lays' Cafeteria and Grocery Store on 38th Street, west of where The Meadows would rise years later, as well as various other jobs. And in spite of her background, Connie was determined to succeed as a woman in a male-dominated work force. She got a job at Wasson's Department Store in Indianapolis and made enough of an impression that she was promoted to head cashier.

Anyone that spent time around her knew Connie was smart. There was no doubt about that. She continually looked for a better opportunity that would give her the safety and security she so desperately craved. She had a difficult time staying with anything for a long period of time. Her intense desire to succeed was always present. It was manifested by her work ethic.

It was also manifested by her notoriously short temper she could turn on and off like a light switch.

Then, in pursuit of that elusive success, security and acceptance, she made a decision in 1941 that would change the lives of so many.

She accepted a position as a file clerk at Eli Lilly and Company in Indianapolis.

Chapter 5

"A satellite scientist said yesterday space travelers of the future would have to be shielded by about 100 pounds of lead each against a strange reservoir of intense radiation developing around the earth.

United Press Report
May 2, 1958

1958 couldn't come soon enough for young lawyer Tom. There would be another election for Criminal Court #1 in 1958 and he wanted it more than anything.

Luckily, in the meantime, Phil Bayt was still the judge in Municipal Court #3. He continued to support Tom, time and time again appointing him as judge pro tem in his court. Bayt would continue as the judge in that court until 1955, when, once again, Bayt would run for mayor of Indianapolis. However, this time, state law would not allow him to keep his job as a judge and run for a different political office. Luckily for Tom, Bayt's replacement, Patrick Barton, kept up Bayt's custom of appointing him judge pro tem in his court.

Tom fell in love with the feeling of sitting behind the bench in the expansive, impressive courtroom. Municipal Court #3 was physically much like Criminal Court #1 and commanded respect for the person sitting at the helm. The more Faulconer was appointed judge pro tem, the more he realized that he wanted to be a judge full-time.

Bayt ran a spirited campaign in the 1955 race. He easily won the primary and, as the candidate for mayor of Indianapolis for the Democratic Party, was elected to his first term, having been appointed earlier.

By now, Bayt and his disciples were feeling their oats. They had toppled the leadership of both the state and national Democratic Party, and now, they had recaptured the mayor's office.

But, once again, in a pattern becoming too familiar, Tom's fortunes would wane.

When Phil Bayt won the election in 1955, his longtime support of the young lawyer abruptly stopped. Whether this was conscious or unconscious, no one really knows. In exchange for his support of Bayt over the last five years, Tom was optimistic that he would be appointed to some post in the mayor's administration.

That never happened.

At first, Tom was bitter that he had been abandoned by the man who had served as his mentor for the past several years. However, in time, he would come to realize how much he owed Bayt and that, in truth, Bayt owed him nothing.

But the relationship of Phil Bayt and Tom Faulconer was not over yet, not by a long shot. They would meet again a few short years later in a way that neither of them could have imagined in 1955.

In late 1955, Robert O'Neal was still the elected sheriff in Marion County and was quite popular in the Indianapolis community. He had developed a fairly close friendship with Tom, the young Democrat lawyer. They would spend lunch hours in the small kitchen in the Marion County jail discussing politics and all of the ways they would change the world. When O'Neal realized that Bayt was not going to appoint Tom to a position in the administration, O'Neal alerted him to a position on the Indiana State Election Board.

The timing couldn't have been better.

The Indiana State Election board was a bipartisan committee with only three members. A Democrat was appointed and a Republican was appointed. The governor of the state served as the third member.

This time, thankfully, the position had not been filled and the governor, a Republican, on the recommendation of the State Democratic Chairman, agreed to appoint the young lawyer as the Democrat member of the board.

The committee had regular meetings at the Governor's office in the State Capitol. These afforded the opportunity for Tom to expand his reputation, not to mention the chance to get to know Governor George Craig on a personal basis.

More importantly at the moment was the $200 per month salary.

By June of 1956, with Sheriff O'Neal's assistance, Tom had also been elected Secretary of the Democratic State Committee. This was not a particularly powerful, important or well-known committee position. But it did have one particular feature that was very important at the time.

It paid $200 per month as well. It also provided plenty of statewide exposure.

Not forgetting the roots of his past successes, as the next few years passed he kept active in Indiana Democrat politics. He became a ward chairman (legitimately) and anxiously awaited the opportunity to run for Criminal Court #1 again.

Unbelievably, he waited too long.

By the time the aspiring judge got around to preparing his filing to run for the court, another Democrat had filed. Since the other candidate had the backing of the party, Tom knew his candidacy for the same office could serve as a wedge in the fragile party unity.

He decided not to run for Criminal Court #1 in 1958.

At the time, there was another criminal court in Marion County, Criminal Court #2. But there weren't many lawyers interested in challenging for the seat behind this bench. Criminal Court #2 had been created in 1947 to help ease the growing caseload in Criminal Court #1 and the first judge of the new court was appointed that same year.

Venerable Judge Saul Rabb had been there ever since.

Judge Rabb may have looked the part of a judge, but his gruff style and demeanor had alienated more than a few attorneys who appeared in his court. Although they would deny it, some of the deputy prosecutors had even found ways to manipulate the filing system to assure that their cases would be filed in Criminal Court #1 rather than face the sometimes unpredictable Saul Rabb.

Through the 1950s, new criminal charges were assigned to either Criminal Court #1 or Criminal Court #2. When Criminal Court #2 was created, a plan was implemented that directed the clerk of the courts to assign criminal cases to alternating courts. For example, the first case would be assigned to Criminal Court #1, the second to Criminal Court #2, the third to #1, the fourth to #2 and so on.

Criminal cases were filed by the prosecutor's office. Not long after this system was implemented, deputy prosecutors began deliberately placing criminal filings in order. More complex cases, in which the prosecutor may have a more difficult time were filed first, third, fifth, etc. Those cases that were clear winners or clear losers for the prosecutor's office were filed second, fourth, sixth, etc. Consequently, tougher, more complex cases generally ended up in Criminal Court #1.

After several years, the caseload for Criminal Court #1 was much greater than in Criminal Court #2. Simpler cases are typically plea-bargained or dismissed and disposed of quickly. The tougher cases tend to drag on for months, even years. Therefore, with new cases being assigned at an equal rate, the docket for Criminal Court #1 was understandably heavier than that in Criminal Court #2.

So the judges revised the system in the mid-1950s. the new system required the prosecutor's office, when filing criminal charges, to file the first 100 in Criminal Court #1, the second 100 in Criminal Court #2 and so on through each year. This assured a more equal distribution of cases and helped prevent the prosecutor from picking the more favorable court.

The system worked well, and, eventually, the caseload in the two courts balanced out.

No matter how unpredictable, Judge Rabb of Criminal Court #2 was Republican through and through. And his party was not about to relinquish control of Criminal Court #2. At least not without a heck of a fight.

Every election for the job of judge in Criminal Court #2 since 1947 had been a formality. No one had seriously challenged the entrenched jurist. And, in 1958, no one really wanted to.

Hesitantly, Tom Faulconer considered challenging the long-time judge for the Criminal Court #2 seat. Finally, realizing that he would otherwise be forced to wait four more years for another chance at Criminal Court #1, Faulconer filed his paperwork to become a Democrat candidate against the older, imposing Saul Rabb.

Tom Faulconer wasn't the only Democrat who filed, but he was the only one who had the party backing. He was also the only one with any chance at all of making a run for the job. His primary opponent was a 55 year-old lawyer named Charlie Steger. Charlie Steger had been active only on the periphery of politics and had never sought public office before.

No one gave Steger much of a chance to survive the primary. He didn't.

Faulconer won the primary with over 71% of the vote.

Once again, the tougher fight was yet to come and everyone knew it.

While all the party infighting was going on in the mid-1950's, Connie Nicholas felt as though she had finally gotten her rocky life on track. Or so it seemed.

By 1942, she had met and married a man named Ray Keifer. After just a few years of marriage, she divorced him in the late 1940's. In the mid-1950s, she married again. But, by 1958, her second marriage had basically dissolved itself. She and her husband had gone their separate ways and weren't even living together anymore. Curt Nicholas would file for divorce that year and it would be granted without argument. But, believe it or not, she was actually quite happy at this stage of her life. She had met someone new with whom she had fallen madly in love.

While working at Eli Lilly, Connie's affections were pursued doggedly by another employee. He was handsome, charming and many years her senior. When hired, she was a 27 year-old secretary at the time, having worked her way from the file room in the months preceding. The 37 year-old, suitor was a sales representative for Lilly, but was already on the fast track. He would move up quickly, was the conventional wisdom. It turned out to be true.

Connie claimed to have resisted his advances for almost two years. However, the two had a chance meeting outside a hotel in downtown Indianapolis one day that led to the man buying her a drink at the hotel bar. That first meeting was innocuous and platonic. But the many more meetings that would follow would escalate the swelling passion that was smoldering between them.

By the mid-1950's they were a bona fide couple. They could be seen together shopping and attending social events every Thursday night. They celebrated birthdays together, and eventually traveled together to places like Chicago and even Havana, Cuba, all on business trips paid for by Lilly, and registering in hotels as husband and wife in the image conscious 50's.

When her new man was around, Connie was ecstatic. The handsome, fit, caring man represented to Connie everything she hadn't had for the first 27 years of her life. He was, at least locally, well-known, showered her with affection, made her feel loved and even paid many of her bills for her. In short, he worshipped her.

Eventually, she gave him a key to her apartment and he came and went as he pleased. After all, for the last three years, he had paid the rent—a year at a time, lump sum.

A happier couple couldn't be found in Indianapolis in the 1950's.

They even talked about a wedding date. The specific date was not set, but they would marry in 1961. He had some personal issues to tend to before they could get married. But they would marry, he continually assured her. She believed him with all her heart.

In 1958, Connie survived on the knowledge that Forrest Teel would be hers in just three short years.

Unfortunately, in 1958, the now 54 year-old Teel had one more thing that Connie would have just as soon he didn't. He had a wife of 26 years and a 14 year-old son.

Chapter 6

"Postal rates went up today. It now costs 4 cents an ounce for 1st class mail, 7 cents for air mail, 3 cents for a postcard and 5 cents for air mail postcards."
Indianapolis Star
August 1, 1958

On most mornings in July, at 4:10 AM, the sun would, by now, have cleared the horizon and started the warm-up inevitable in the Midwest. But there would be no sun the morning of July 31, 1958.

With robbery ruled out as a motive, it was clear that someone was mad enough at Forrest Teel to want him dead. Captain Smiley of the homicide division of the Indianapolis Police Department was arriving at the Teel house on exclusive Washington Boulevard to tell Teel's wife of 26 years that someone had succeeded. The Captain's car was the only one moving in the early morning glare from the black asphalt of Washington Boulevard.

Washington Boulevard is one of the country's most beautiful streets. It was and is picturesque. It is an eclectic mix of stately homes built in the early part of the twentieth century. By the 1920's, Washington Boulevard had secured its place among Indianapolis neighborhoods.

Even a visitor unfamiliar with its residents and reputation would have been able to sense its wealth and prestige in 1958 Indianapolis. Meticulous detail to landscaping and shiny new Cadillacs, Chyslers, Lincolns and Oldsmobiles with stark whitewalls and glistening chrome bumpers, were a sure giveaway.

The police get to know certain parts of any town. The Indianapolis Police had made entirely too many trips to those familiar parts of town to deliver news of shootings and stabbings. But Washington Boulevard was definitely new territory. As if on cue, the thickening clouds released a steady rain during the detective's trip to the Teel home.

The story of the Teels was an unlikely one in the 1930s. Continental travel was time consuming and difficult in pre-interstate America. International travel was arduous and uncommon. Yet the Teels would meet in a foreign land, two Americans displaced and out of place.

Mary Elizabeth Roddy was actually a Texas native. And although she had claimed Texas as her home since her birth in 1913, she had spent precious little time there. Her father was a financial analyst for the United States Government and as part of his regular assignments, was regularly sent to foreign lands. Often these trips would last weeks, months and even longer. Like the good family man he was, he took his wife and daughter with him when he could.

1932 found the Roddys encamped in Colombia, South America. Mary Elizabeth, now 21 years old, cherished the few friendships she developed with other United States citizens. While she easily and understandably could have opted out of traveling with her parents to her dad's overseas assignments, shy, uncertain Mary Elizabeth preferred the comfort and security of her family to the lonesome family home in Texas.

Forrest Teel had taken another path completely. After graduation with admirable marks from college, in 1926, Forrest accepted a position as a sales representative for the Eli Lilly and Company in Indianapolis, Indiana. His first job assignment was in Chanute, Kansas, a town in southeastern Kansas of just a few thousand residents. The town was still growing in the 1920's, having just been wired for electricity in 1916. However, it was a prime location for a traveling salesman being situated nearly equidistant between Topeka and Wichita in Kansas, Springfield, Missouri and Tulsa, Oklahoma. Forrest invaded the staunchly conservative company armed with considerable charm and charisma. He also had a big ego as well. In order to groom the young Forrest for later assignments at the company, he was moved frequently from area to area, division to division in order to broaden his perspective and overall understanding of the pharmaceutical business.

By the early 1930s, Forrest Teel was working in Colombia, South America, too.

Not long after the Roddy family arrived, Mary Elizabeth met the handsome and charming Teel though mutual friends. The prospect of having another US citizen to talk to and spend time with delighted them both. Soon, they were fast friends and soon after, they were more than that.

The Teels had married in 1932. Soon after the marriage, Forrest received his next assignment. He was to move back to Indianapolis to work in the home office of the company. Mary Elizabeth dutifully followed him back to their new home.

The first impression of the supervisors of the dapper, confident young man had been correct. Forrest progressed quickly on the corporate organizational chart, acquiring more prestige, responsibility for a larger staff and a much larger paycheck along the way.

Mary Elizabeth was not accustomed to wealth and luxury. She would have been just as happy to have a small house in the suburbs with the picket fence and a dog. But Forrest was ambitious in everything he did. Image was paramount. Soon, the Teels began acquiring many of the trappings of his success.

Not the least of which was their home. One of the grandest homes in the city, it was located on one of the most exclusive parts of Washington Boulevard.

The Teels became fixtures on the burgeoning Indianapolis scene. Rumors abounded that Mrs. Teel did not enjoy the heavy social schedule of her husband.

Nonetheless, without fail, she appeared by his side, going out of her way to be cordial and make others feel comfortable.

As the policemen located the deep red brick house at 5921 Washington Boulevard, they were immediately struck by the ivy disciplined into a random climb from the ground, framing the awning-covered windows and the arched portico supported by delicate fluted columns that framed the front door. The large trees in the yard were irrefutable evidence of years of professional landscape planning and maintenance. And although the hedge that lined the westside of the driveway still had it's bright green spring growth jutting several inches in all directions, the property reeked of wealth, money and status.

As the detectives left their car parked on the street and walked the straight, concrete sidewalk to the front door, each felt his pulse quicken. This was a necessary part of the job. But they suddenly felt underpaid.

No one expects a knock on the door at 4:00 in the morning. But on Washington Boulevard in Indianapolis in 1958, 48 year-old Mary Elizabeth Teel trustingly opened the door to find two men who quickly identified themselves as Captain Michael Smiley and Inspector Carl Schmidt both from the Indianapolis Police Department Homicide Division.

The officers found themselves face-to-face with a small, dark haired woman with a shy, pleasant smile. Her thick, shoulder-length hair and small, delicate features conspired to produce an appearance younger than her age. She seemed more like a schoolgirl than the wife of a powerful corporate executive.

As Forrest and Mary Elizabeth's 14-year-old son, Tommy slept peacefully in an upstairs bedroom innocently oblivious to the visitors downstairs, the police officers delivered the worst news a wife can ever expect to get about her husband. Forrest was dead.

The officers briefed Mrs. Teel in the living room of the executive's large home. They looked around at a décor that betrayed the couple's enviable lifestyle. But the officers could not know that they were only seeing a part of the story. In an attempt to satisfy Forrest's desire to have the latest and greatest of everything he owned, he insisted that the house be redecorated frequently. Styles from last year were simply unacceptable. Consequently, the Teel's were known to redecorate often, another perk made possible by Forrest's large income. Their friends with less generous incomes were often the beneficiaries of these exercises, the recipients of the Teels' cast-offs.

Surprisingly, many times, the police find that relatives of victims of violent deaths are most helpful just after being told the bad news. Before the reality of the situation settles on a relative, they are likely to be able to think somewhat clearly. Besides, in more than a few murder cases, the relatives are involved. It was important for the policemen to deliver the news quickly and to gauge Mrs. Teel's reaction.

The officers hoped to uncover something by talking with Mary Elizabeth Teel that morning.

The officers met the classic good news/bad news situation. While Mrs. Teel was able to think clearly and converse coherently with the detectives, she was unable to fill any of the gaps in the theories that were developing to explain her husband's death. No, she could offer no reason why her husband was in the Meadows area at 1:00 am. She didn't know who would want her husband dead. She had no idea who would kill him.

She gave the two men a picture of a successful 26-year marriage filled with happiness and love.

The men left the house doubting that Mrs. Teel had anything to do with the murder of her husband, both wondering what had happened and hoping for some help.

And, despite years of hardening police work, they couldn't help but feel sorry for Mrs. Teel and her son.

The sun shining translucent through gathering rain clouds was well above the horizon now and Washington Boulevard was hosting its first traffic of the morning as they returned to their car.

Anyone who has watched a police drama on television knows it isn't uncommon for homicide detectives to work very odd hours. Indeed, because clues vanish so quickly in most cases and the likelihood that a murder will be solved decreases rapidly in the hours immediately after the killing, many detectives find themselves working 24 hours or more straight. It is often not a conscious decision to continue. They simply lose track of time.

Murders don't happen on a schedule. Like a bloodhound on a scent, a detective just might work a case until he physically and mentally can't go on anymore.

These days, not many marriages and even fewer relationships survive the career of the homicide detective.

The detectives working the murder of Forrest Teel had several unanswered questions. The most obvious was who shot him. But they also had other questions, the answers to which would hopefully lead them to that ultimate answer and solve the case.

The biggest of the remaining questions: Who was driving the other car?

But, even that question turned out to be complicated for the lawmen.

Eyewitnesses are given unbelievable weight in a court of law. Juries routinely convict on eyewitness testimony with little corroborating evidence. Yet studies have consistently shown, and police officers will confirm, eyewitnesses are very often mistaken. In fact, eyewitness testimony is, in reality, among the least reliable evidence.

In the case of the murder of Forrest Teel, the detectives received just such conflicting stories from some of the witnesses they interviewed.

Some of the witnesses reported seeing one person leaving the scene, others reported two. Some reported a blue and white Oldsmobile, others, a cream-colored Cadillac. In still other accounts, the Oldsmobile was a Chevrolet.

It seemed the only undeniable constant in the story was that Forrest Teel was dead.

As the policemen left the big house on Washington Boulevard, Mary Elizabeth Teel, known to her family and friends as "Betty," sat in her living room contemplating the sudden change in her life.

Yesterday, she was a socialite, she had awakened a widow.

By almost all accounts, their marriage had been one straight from a storybook. They had been married for twenty-six years, they were regularly featured guests at parties and dinners in the Indianapolis area. They were literally the picture of happiness and success with one of the largest homes in Indianapolis, new cars, a handsome young son. Only one thing was missing from the life of Betty Teel. And because of it, she was dreadfully unhappy.

While Mrs. Teel attempted to recover from the devastating news she had just received, at least one other person was feeling similar pain. A pretty, petite redhead awoke early on July 31, showered and readied herself for work as a secretary at Eli Lilly. It was a familiar routine she had followed the previous four days that week, preceded by countless others. This morning was tougher, though, as she had not gone to bed until very late the night before.

She strode leisurely from the bathroom to the bedroom, dressed for work and walked through the living room to the front door of her apartment to get her copy of the Indianapolis Star, the city's morning newspaper. She was in no hurry, she was up early despite her late evening, and had plenty of time to make the twenty-minute commute to work.

As she opened the door of her one-bedroom apartment, the headline of the paper stopped her in her tracks and made her heart pound violently. Her body felt tight. "Executive Shot to Death—Lilly Vice President Killed in Auto," screamed the dark black letters. Just below the headlines was a black and white publicity picture, one and a half inches by two inches of Forrest Teel. She glanced through the hallways of her apartment building, quickly backed into her apartment, her shaking hands holding the newspaper, and shut the door behind her.

The sometime model stood in her living room, reading the first few paragraphs detailing the murder that had happened just a few feet from the door to her apartment building in the Meadowbrook Apartments. Incredibly, she had heard nothing the night before.

Quickly, she tossed the paper on a coffee table in the living room, finished getting dressed, climbed into her 1953 blue Chevrolet and raced from the area on the rainy streets of Indianapolis.

A few minutes later, she parked her car in the company parking lot and walked purposefully to her desk at the Eli Lilly and Company. Most of the other employees were still an hour or two away from starting the last of their daily toils for the week. Not waiting for an elevator, she climbed the couple of flights of stairs to her floor and hurried to her metal desk. The young lady quickly removed all her personal items from her desk, recklessly tossing pictures and keepsakes into her purse and paper sacks, emptied the drawers and took a quick look around for any stray items she may have forgotten.

Satisfied nothing was left, she left the building.

Only one other employee in the young woman's department was there at this early hour. She was a good friend, even playing in the same bridge club with her. But the pretty, young girl was much too focused and frightened to even acknowledge her friend.

Beautiful Laura Mowrer, a 29-year-old secretary at Lilly, would never return to work there again.

Her supervisor would receive her resignation letter a few days later.

Her lawyer would receive a call almost immediately.

In 1958, Judge Saul Rabb was the 55 year-old incumbent in Criminal Court #2. The difference between Rabb and Tom Faulconer's primary opponent he had so easily defeated, though, was experience. Rabb was a committed Republican who worked tirelessly on behalf of his party. He had formerly been the chief deputy prosecutor for the county and had now been a judge for almost nine years. He was active in the community and, from outward appearance, apparently, well liked, although there was a considerable contingent of lawyers who may have argued with that perception.

Everyone knew, beating Judge Rabb would be difficult.

Once again, Tom Faulconer knew that his fortunes were most likely tied to the party. In addition to campaigning on his own behalf, he prayed for a Democrat landslide.

And for most of the campaign season, it looked as though his dream was a long shot at best. The Democrats were still fighting for control at the local level and the focus of the struggle was in an unlikely place, the Marion County Prosecutor's office.

In 1958, there wasn't a mayoral election. But nonetheless, Indianapolis got a new mayor. Charles Boswell was appointed to complete the short remaining term of the departing mayor, Phil Bayt.

Phil Bayt quit the mayor's job to run for prosecutor. While campaigning, Bayt supported himself as the new head of the Better Business Bureau.

Now, on the surface, a move such as this would seem quite odd. But, again, this was Indianapolis in the 1950's. The mayor's job, while prestigious, was just not the springboard it sometimes is today. Bayt was still able to complete his duties as mayor and operate his law practice in his spare time. The prosecutor's job, on the other hand, could be a full-time position with lots of clout and lots of exposure.

By now, the 48 year-old Bayt had already lived a colorful life. But he wasn't done yet.

Another faction of the Democratic Party would run Owen Mullin for the Prosecutor's job. The 40 year-old Mullin was a standard figure in Indiana politics. He also was a good candidate. He was a veteran, a graduate of the Indiana University Law School and a solid family man with five children. Currently, he was county chairman for the party.

The strange part was, Owen Mullin didn't seem to want the job.

The Democrats had their slating meeting on Saturday, April 21, 1958. Phil Bayt had the support he needed and won the party's nomination. However, a hardcore group of ward chairmen was not about to give up. They attempted to draft Owen Mullin as their candidate. They were ready to "buck" the slate.

Owen Mullin, for one, seemed less than enthused. "Apparently, I'm the only member of the [Owen] Mullin faction that's going to vote for Phil Bayt," he was quoted as saying.

The apparently loyal Mullin promised to support the slate.

Two days later, all the wounds were healed and the Democrats professed unity once again.

Then, a week later, after some philosophical disagreements with Bayt, Owen Mullin had changed his mind and announced his candidacy against Phil Bayt.

The renewal of Mullin's candidacy made the primary election a fight between city hall and the county organization. The election would be a referendum on just who would captain the Democratic ship in the coming years.

Everyone claims to hate negative campaigning. But negative campaigning is nothing new. Even in 1958, the two came out slugging.

Mullin claimed he was back in the race because "you can't be nice to Mayor Bayt."

Bayt charged that Mullin's actions proved that he "is insincere and that his word means nothing."

The bitter contest went to the wire. It provided not only interesting news copy, but also spurred one of the largest turnouts in Indiana primary election history.

Pre-primary election polls consistently showed a race that would go the distance. It was too close to call, trumpeted the newspapers.

But in the end, the vote was anticlimactic. Bayt won by a margin of over 2 to 1.

So, three years after their unexplained parting, Phil Bayt and Tom Faulconer would once again be united. This time as Democratic candidates in the election of 1958.

Chapter 7

"After questioning several persons in the vicinity of the murder scene, detectives today reported they had not learned anything 'significant.'"
Indianapolis Star
July 31, 1958

The headlines on Friday morning broke the story of a mystery gunman who had taken the life of one of Indianapolis' most prominent citizens. The details that were available were hastily compiled, mildly inaccurate and read with unbelievable intensity citywide. The ambush of Forrest Teel became the topic of conversation at breakfast tables and coffee breaks citywide. Opinions were formed and rumors were circulated on the thinnest of authority.

Luckily, several people very important to the case would also read that morning's news. One of them was cab driver Wesley Miller.

Captain Smiley took a call from the cab driver who was driving in the area of The Meadows just after midnight in the early morning hours of July 31. The 28 year-old Miller was driving his State Cab to pick up a fare at the Sam's Subway restaurant in the Meadows. One of the waitresses had just gotten off work and needed a ride home. As cabby Miller neared the restaurant, he was flagged down by two men standing alongside a cream-colored Cadillac.

Miller stopped to see what they wanted.

The men told him that there had been an auto accident and asked the cab driver to call police.

Cautious, Miller discounted their story and drove on. Even in 1958, Miller was concerned for his safety driving a cab in the middle of the night.

It was not until he had picked up his fare and was leaving the Meadowbrook Shopping Center that Miller noticed a crowd gathering around the white Cadillac as it rested against the utility pole.

At that point, Miller realized that the men were telling the truth and he did call the police. He was told that they had already been notified. The dispatcher did not ask for, nor did the cab driver offer any further information.

Immediately, Captain Smiley issued an alert to all police officers. The crude speakers mounted in all the patrol cars blared the instruction to watch for the two men in the cream-colored Cadillac. Even though the descriptions were not particularly complete - one was described as about 30, 5 feet 10 inches tall with heavy, dark hair and wearing a blue suit, and the other was described as about 30, short and slightly built - the fact is that there would not be too many cream-colored Cadillacs in the Indianapolis area with occupants that fit the descriptions.

The information was also released in the next edition of the Indianapolis News. Almost immediately, a 30-ish man with dark, heavy hair named Leonard Larman came forward to admit that he was the one the cab driver had described. He and a friend were driving in the area with their wives, saw the accident happen and stopped the cab driver.

However, believing everything was under control, they left the scene.

To most, in the clarity of hindsight, this account seemed very strange. But the pair was investigated thoroughly and excluded as suspects, simply in the wrong place at the wrong time.

The mystery of the two men in the cream-colored Cadillac was solved.

That still left the mystery of the blue and white Oldsmobile and whoever was inside. The police focused their attention on this lead. The killer was most likely inside that car.

But before any of the patrolmen could locate the blue and white getaway car, help would arrive from another source.

In a matter of hours, another phone call was transferred to Captain Smiley. This time, the caller was reluctant to identify himself. However, he did offer some very important information. "If Teel was shot by a .25 caliber, I know who did it," he said.

In truth, the caller did not *know* who did it. What he had was a strong hunch. But the police wouldn't have cared about his hunch.

He told the police that they needed to look for a woman named Connie Nicholas.

After some prompting, he eventually did identify himself. His name was Ralph Gano. He was the owner of the B & G Swap Shop in Indianapolis and he had sold Connie Nicholas a .25 caliber pistol nearly two weeks before. Upon hearing that the victim was shot with a .25 caliber weapon, Gano had a feeling she just might be the shooter.

In fact, Gano didn't just sell her the gun. Connie Nicholas had charmed and flirted her way into free shooting lessons. Ralph Gano had taught her to shoot.

Gano was an attractive, dark haired man who sported the quasi-military burr haircut so common in the post World War II era. He was in his mid-to late-thirties and was prone to wearing t-shirts a size or two too small. But most importantly, he knew how to handle a gun.

Really, the B & G Swap Shop was a bit of a misnomer. It was little more than a pawn shop. The fact is, B & G Swap Shop was a great place to buy a gun and guns were its only real business.

Pawn shops were favorite haunts of criminals and favorite targets of police. Ralph Gano didn't want to invite any more police to the shop than he had to. But he quickly realized the severity of the case and called Captain Smiley with his information.

Early in July, 1958, Ralph Gano was working at the B & G Swap Shop. The store was located across town from The Meadows area. For someone like Connie Nicholas who lived a short distance from The Meadows, the B & G Swap Shop was certainly an odd choice. She would have to make a fairly time-consuming trek to the store on West 30th Street in a time before interstate highways made cross-town travel an everyday occurrence. She would also pass several other places that sold guns along the way.

On July 10, the phone rang at the B & G Swap Shop. A female voice on the other end asked a simple question. The caller wanted to know if she could buy a gun.

Gano assured the caller that she could purchase from a wide range of firearms. She thanked him and hung up.

Gano remembered that phone call for a couple of reasons. First, in 1958, seldom did a woman want to buy a gun. Second, most of the business at the store came from those in the neighboring areas. They would simply stop by and look.

Plus, there were multitudes of places to buy guns in Indianapolis. A phone call asking such a question was odd. It wasn't like they were hard to find.

Consequently, Gano remembered the call.

Two days later, a customer entered the store. As usual, Gano, the owner, was working the counter. The customer was a petite woman, dressed quite conservatively. She appeared to be in her 40s with short, wiry dark hair. She was slender, somewhat attractive and professionally dressed. She tried to look confident as she entered the store, but Gano knew immediately that she was pretending. She strode to the counter and told the clerk that she was interested in a gun for personal protection. In fact, she mentioned that she had called a couple of days before.

Gano made the connection to the phone call two days prior.

Gano showed the woman several handguns. It was clear she knew little about firearms. She was uncomfortable. She asked very basic questions. Consequently, the clerk took considerable time explaining the advantages and disadvantages of each.

The customer repeatedly told the clerk that she needed the gun for protection during a trip she was planning to California. Gano wondered why she kept repeating that information. It was as if she wanted to make sure he heard it—and remembered it. Maybe she did. Regardless, it worked.

The customer seemed to gravitate to a small .22 caliber model. However, she left the store without making a purchase.

On July 14, the door opened again. The lady interested in a gun had returned.

She presented Gano with a check, already completed, to purchase the .22 she had been eyeing. But while the clerk was processing her transaction, her attention turned to a different gun in a nearby case.

She asked to see it.

Gano reluctantly presented the woman a rare .25 caliber French-made pistol. Its construction was quite unique. It had no visible hammer and fit in the palm of a normal-sized hand. The barrel was only two inches long. The entire gun was less than six inches in length. It was dark gray in color and had what appeared to be pearl insets in the handle. It was very lightweight, perhaps slightly over a pound.

The gun had no trigger guard. Instead, the comparatively long trigger folded up into the underside of the gun.

There was a safety lever on the left side and a small metal fin protruding from the top to serve as a site.

Upon examining the smaller, more compact pistol, the customer changed her mind. She wanted the .25 caliber weapon instead. The fact that it was considerably more expensive, due mainly to its rarity, made no difference. Connie wanted that gun and no other. Gano tried his best to steer her back to the .22 caliber. The French revolver wouldn't be as reliable, he assured her.

Connie insisted on the pricier, .25 caliber model.

To Gano, it was definitely a "woman's gun."

Her choice of the rare .25 caliber pistol would come back to haunt her.

In 1958, Indiana required a three-day waiting period for the purchase of a handgun. This was nothing more than a cooling-off period. No background checks were made or other security measures taken. So by July 17, Connie Nicholas had a gun and a paper sack with 12 bullets as she left the B & G Swap Shop.

Connie was charismatic and she had learned to turn that on when she wanted to. Once she made the purchase, she began to flirt with Gano. The childhood street education of Connie Nicholas had taught her how to get what she wanted. She charmed the handsome clerk into giving her free private lessons with the new weapon. She would return later that night for the first one.

During the last two weeks of July, Gano and Connie would meet four more times. The first meetings would involve basic instruction, but the firearm was not discharged. The last two meetings took place in a remote location just outside the city limits of Indianapolis where first Gano, then Connie actually shot the gun into a sand mound.

That training would come in handy very soon.

By the morning of August 1, 1958, on the advice of the gun dealer, the homicide detectives were on their way to the apartment of a 44 year-old divorcee named Connie Nicholas.

4505 Marcy Lane is part of an all-brick apartment complex located on the northside of Indianapolis, just about two miles west of the Meadows. It has the look of a military compound in a way, comprised of several two-story brick buildings set at different angles among a large lawn that sets the complex apart from busy 46th Street.

In 1958, the driveways and carports were hidden to outsiders which only served to reinforce the militaristic look of the area.

In truth, the apartments were quite nice, located in a safe area, and reasonably priced such that young professionals were among its more prevalent tenants.

The detectives arrived at 4505 Marcy Lane to find a key taped to the door of the apartment along with a note.

Captain Smiley carefully removed the note from the tape suspending it from the door. He wasn't sure what to expect. But once he read it, he felt sure he was on the right track.

Captain Smiley was holding in his hands a suicide note apparently authored by Connie Nicholas. Although the men could not be certain of its authenticity, they couldn't take any chances.

The first thing the detectives thought was that their now-prime suspect just might be inside the apartment, possibly in the throes of death. Justifiably, most would agree, they inserted the key in the lock, opened the front door and entered.

Once inside, they found a neat, well-kept, 4-room apartment, littered with a gold mine of evidence regarding the murder of Forrest Teel.

As the detectives scoured her apartment, they found they didn't have to look very hard for items of interest.

In addition to the suicide note found on the apartment door, the detectives found several other suicide notes on a secretary desk in the dining room and scattered around other parts of the neat apartment. They also found a love letter written to Forrest Teel.

The letter pleaded with him to explain why he had broken off their relationship over a simple argument.

Perhaps Forrest Teel was not the family man that the community thought he was.

The police also discovered a pair of men's slippers and a bathrobe in a chair in the living room. "Please return to Mr. Forrest Teel, 5921 Washington Boulevard," read a typed note on top of them.

After a complete search of the apartment, the homicide division had plenty of new information and a definite link between the occupant of the apartment and the victim. But they still didn't have what they needed most: Connie Nicholas.

Another alert was put out to all police officers. Connie Nicholas had to be found.

And, again fate would be kind to Captain Smiley and his men.

Chapter 8

"A typical family man, making $4,500 per year, will pay 31.8% of that for taxes."
Tax Foundation as Reported in the
New York Daily News
April 4, 1959

The daylight hours of July 31, 1958 offered no relief from the midsummer heat. The temperature in the mid-80s and the high humidity conspired to create conditions just right for rain. The precipitation would end by mid-day, but the mugginess of the high humidity remained. This was pretty typical late July/early August weather in Indiana.

After the rain, during the height of the heat, with the sun glowing translucent in the sky, a lone car with a lone occupant drove slowly down the rough dirt road that paralleled the Fall Creek.

Some locals liked to call this stretch lovers' lane.

The motorist noticed a blue coupe parked next to the creek. The blue 1955 Chevrolet had a white painted hardtop. It sat in several inches of mud and was quite a distance from the roadway. From his perspective, the motorist saw no one in the car. Understandably assuming the car was abandoned, the motorist phoned police at his next opportunity and reported an abandoned car by Fall Creek.

The call came into the police at just after 5:00 PM. But a routine call of an abandoned car is very low priority to a police agency. A Marion County Sheriff's deputy was not dispatched to the scene until after 8:00 that evening.

When his cruiser rolled up to the scene, Deputy William Butler had to leave his own patrol car to investigate for fear he would get his car stuck in the mud just as the Chevrolet had apparently become stuck.

As the effect of the pending dusk was exaggerated by the tall oak and pine trees that lined Fall Creek, the deputy routinely shined his police-issue flashlight inside the car expecting to see an empty automobile. Perhaps it had been stolen and left there by the thief. He certainly didn't expect to see a woman, apparently unconscious.

Shocked to see someone in the car, he looked closer, careful not to touch the car. The woman didn't move and he presumed the woman was dead and didn't want to contaminate the crime scene.

A closer inspection changed the deputy's mind. There were tears on the woman's cheek. In the deputy's words, "Dead people don't cry."

Butler opened the car door and confirmed that the woman, clad in a fashionable pink dress, was unconscious but alive. He used the radio in his car to call for an ambulance.

In a matter of minutes, for the second time in less than 24 hours, the ambulance from General Hospital in Indianapolis was racing toward the scene, the mechanical siren screaming a warning to other motorists.

In the meantime, the deputy surveyed the scene. The victim was a petite woman, apparently in her early to mid-40s. She was turned in the bench seat toward the passenger door. Her legs were tucked beneath her on the seat in a quasi-fetal position. Both hands were resting atop one another on the back of the front seat. Her head rested on top of the seat, slightly turned to the left such that her right eye was resting on her hands. There was a thermos and two red capsules on the seat beside the woman.

As it turned out, the only thing that saved the woman's life may have been an intolerant stomach.

The red capsules were potent sleeping pills. She had taken so many pills that her stomach couldn't take it. It had become upset and·she had vomited. This lessened the effect of the pills on her body.

As the ambulance attendants worked, first unsuccessfully, to revive the unconscious woman, then to stabilize her condition for transport to the hospital, the deputy looked around the car for some identification. The registration was in the glove compartment. The name on the official registration meant nothing to the deputy. He recorded her name on his report and went about his business for the evening.

Connie Nicholas had been found.

Deputy Butler also made a careful search of the scene around the car. At this point, he knew virtually nothing of the circumstances that brought the woman here. He found nothing.

Unfortunately, Connie's prognosis was not good. Upon arrival at General Hospital, she remained comatose through the next day. The physician in charge of her care, Dr. Thomas A. Rafalski, announced the following day that Mrs. Nicholas had apparently ingested a large amount of prescription medications.

That was an understatement.

In reality, Connie Nicholas had taken more than 75 prescription sleeping pills, crushed them, and combined them with some pineapple juice. Transporting the concoction in a Thermos, she had ingested the foul paste around noon the day she was found.

The sleeping pills were a prescription drug. They were an Eli Lilly brand. Ironically, they were compliments of Forrest Teel.

After Connie was transported to the hospital, the same hospital in which Forrest Teel lay in a morgue drawer awaiting an autopsy, a further search of Connie's car revealed even more evidence linking her to the crime.

Police found Connie's purse in the car. In the purse were a newspaper photograph of Forrest Teel, two empty medicine vials, and a small paper sack containing seven unfired .25 caliber cartridges.

And a small .25 caliber pistol with four spent rounds and a live round in the chamber.

It appeared that Captain Smiley now had the gun that took the life of Forrest Teel.

And although Captain Smiley believed he had the weapon and the shooter, he still had one very important gap to fill. He still couldn't tell a jury why.

For a while, it looked as though the police and prosecutors might not have to worry about uncovering a motive. The doctors warned the parties involved that Mrs. Nicholas would most likely die from barbiturate poisoning.

Already, police were certain enough of Connie's guilt that a short time later, Captain Smiley announced to the press that Mrs. Nicholas had been found, placed under arrest and, if she died, the case would be closed. General Hospital reported her condition to the curious newspapers and callers as "grave."

But Connie had been a fighter her whole life. And she wouldn't go without a fight this time.

As she lay in her hospital room, ensconced in an oxygen tent and still in her prescription drug-induced coma, a doctor completed the autopsy on Forrest Teel not far away. He concluded that Teel was the victim of three gunshots, one in the neck which lodged near his spine, one in the abdomen that ricocheted off a rib, and one in the hip which lacerated his liver. It was this last bullet that killed him, although not immediately. He had suffered for several minutes.

On August 2, 1958, near the Fall Creek, slightly south of where Connie Nicolas was found two nights before, family and friends gathered at the Flanner and Buchanan Fall Creek Mortuary to say their final good-byes to Forrest Teel, a pillar of the community, gunned down at the height of his career. The Reverend Ernest Lynch, rector of the

Trinity Episcopal Church in Indianapolis officiated, quoting several verses from the Book of Psalms. The service was brief and Teel's body was cremated later that day.

Oddly, no one saw Betty and Tommy Teel, Forrest's wife and son, at the funeral. They remained hidden in the family's room of the mortuary, refusing to speak to mourners.

Again surprising everyone and beating the odds stacked against her, late in the afternoon on Saturday, August 2, 1958, at roughly the same time Forrest Teel was being cremated, Connie came out of her coma. Incredibly, her first words were reportedly, "How is Forrest?"

As she slowly regained consciousness, she realized she was not alone. A detective from the Indianapolis Police Department was assigned to watch her. One of her first sights was of Detective Carl Michaelis.

Detective Michaelis immediately started asking Connie questions.

At first, Connie didn't want to talk. But the Detective kept asking her until she finally relented. "What do you want to talk about?" she asked, as if she didn't know.

Today, such a tactic would be shocking and, most likely, illegal. After all, a defendant must be advised of certain Constitutional rights, such as the right to remain silent, the right to an attorney. But that rule came from a U.S. Supreme Court case called Miranda vs. Arizona. They are accordingly called "Miranda warnings." But the Miranda case was still eight years away. There was no significant legal restriction on interrogations of a witness in 1958.

Connie, in her post-coma haze, would tell the detective how she had lain in wait in Teel's white Cadillac, confronted Forrest Teel and shot him. She didn't say anything about the shooting being accidental. She didn't say anything about being remorseful.

Telling the police she was guilty was bad enough.

As she continued, Connie likely began to feel as though she could manipulate Detective Michaelis in the same way she had manipulated so many others in her life. She began asking him which facts would be most likely to get her acquitted of the crime.

Michaelis was taken aback by the fact that Connie, literally minutes from a coma, was already planning her defense.

What she did next was downright shocking.

Connie packed her hospital room with reporters and told the world that she had killed Forrest Teel.

Chapter 9

"Democrats Sweep State"
Page 1 Headline of the Indianapolis Star
November 5, 1958

Indianapolis was greeted by a picture of a smiling, round face framing thick, black glasses on the front page of the Indianapolis Star on the morning of November 5, 1958. And Phil Bayt had good reason to smile. The former City Controller and Mayor would be the next prosecuting attorney for Marion County Indiana for the next four years.

But more importantly, Thomas J. Faulconer, III would now be known as Judge Faulconer. He had done the impossible. Legendary Saul Rabb was out of a job.

All in all, the Democrats had swept virtually all of the county contests in the general election. But it was far from a landslide. While the Democrats did gain 11 seats in the state legislature and earned a virtual lock on the county, the average margin of victory countywide was less than 3%.

But the only thing that mattered to Tom Faulconer was that the radio had reported his victory the evening before and now there it was in print. It was official. Faulconer was ecstatic.

In the ensuing days, Faulconer received two phone calls at his four-bedroom home on the northeastside of Indianapolis. The first one was from a well-known reporter and then-city editor for the Indianapolis Times newspaper, Irving Leibowitz. Leibowitz was of the old school of reporting. He got right to the point. After offering cursory congratulations, he reminded Faulconer that he couldn't be a judge and keep his part-time political jobs. He demanded to know when Faulconer would resign the Election Board and his party's State Secretary positions.

Days later, the phone rang again. This time, the voice was no one Faulconer recognized.

The caller identified himself as a reporter for the United Press in New York City. He first offered his congratulations on the election victory.

Faulconer accepted the accolade, but in his mind, was baffled. Why would the United Press in New York, New York, care that he had won a judge's job in Marion County, Indiana?

The next words by the caller would answer that question.

"When are you going to set Connie Nicholas for trial?"

Tom Faulconer was stunned.

He had been so wrapped up in the campaign and so focused on beating Saul Rabb, that, although he knew of the Teel murder—everyone in Indianapolis did - he had paid no attention to which court the Connie Nicholas trial had been assigned.

Murder charges had been filed against Connie Nicholas under the relatively new filing system instituted to more equitably balance the caseloads of the two Criminal Courts. Unbeknownst to Faulconer, her case had been assigned to Criminal Court #2.

He had just won the job of trying Connie Nicholas and he didn't even know it.

The new judge in Criminal Court #2 was 35 years old and had never tried a jury trial. His heart began beating harder and a lump appeared in his throat.

Like the dog that catches the car, Faulconer wondered what to do now.

As he thought about the coming months, he found no more comfort. It occurred to him that he had never tried a murder trial. Worse yet, he had never been involved in a murder trial as either prosecutor, defense attorney or even witness.

He had never even seen a murder trial. Now he would have to try his very first one under a public microscope.

In the wake of a violent death, any community goes through an emotional process not unlike the grieving process that the victim's family endures. In the immediate aftermath before explanations are offered, those living in the area where the act took place first worry about their own safety. The possibility of the action being a violent, random attack puts everyone on edge. Doors are locked and curtains are drawn. Rumors travel rapidly.

But once an explanation is offered, or, in many cases, even a plausible theory that potentially disproves the random crime wave scenario, the community transitions to a mode of curiosity.

The Connie Nicholas saga was no exception to this pattern.

By the afternoon of August 2, 1958, as Connie Nicholas awakened from her comatose state of over 36 hours, the city of Indianapolis had already been offered its alternative theory. The residents were certain now that this was no random crime. The July 31 headline of the Indianapolis Times, "Eli Lilly Vice President Slain In His Own Car By Mystery Gunman," was followed the next day by a proclamation of the likely guilt of Connie Nicholas.

And, so, as the Indianapolis community sighed its collective relief at the knowledge that a deranged killer was not stalking the streets in search of his next victim, and as mothers again let their children play outside in the darkness of the Indiana summer nights, the story of the murder of the international vice president of a Fortune 500 company began to spread and became a fascinating story that promised rare glimpses into the lives of the rich and powerful.

Of course 1958 was long before the days of satellite uploads and cellular technology. To get the story, live reporters were sent to the scene. Over the next few days, they came in droves.

Reporters from such remote newspapers as the Billings, Montana Gazette and the Springfield, Missouri News to the powerhouses of the New York Post and even Life magazine and the Chicago Tribune descended on the ill-prepared General Hospital on the near westside of Indianapolis.

They crowded the area just outside the detention ward where Connie Nicholas lay, still trying to make sense of the last 36 hours of her life. An armed police guard stood at the entrance to the ward. The guard was under orders to make sure that Connie Nicholas did not leave.

Amazingly, no one had said anything about letting others in.

Forty years ago hospitals were places for healing. Doctors, nurses and orderlies were the majority of the employees. No one saw the need for spokesmen or public relations people. Consequently, as the media descended on the hospital, the superintendent of the hospital was called to deal with the onslaught.

Dr. Arvine Popplewell did his best to ensure that the sudden influx of paparazzi did not totally disrupt the business of the hospital. However, having never encountered this sort of barrage before, the Dr. was forced to make up the rules as he went along.

The reporters begged Dr. Popplewell to allow them into Connie's room to ask her questions. At first, he simply refused. Dogged members of the press corp pointed out that the decision should be Connie's, not his. Finally, tiring of the constant requests, Dr. Popplewell relented, entered Connie's private prison room and asked her if she would like to talk to the press. She said no.

Over the course of several hours, the reporters continued to badger Dr. Popplewell. Having set the precedent, he felt compelled to continue to ask Connie Nicholas if she wanted to talk to the press.

After repeatedly declining the opportunity, incredibly, in the afternoon of Saturday, August 2, she agreed to let the media in.

At first, Connie Nicholas was a bit overwhelmed by the attention. Her small infirmary room was quickly filled with fifteen or twenty reporters, each jostling for position to see the spurned divorcee who had allegedly killed her married lover in a passionate fit of revenge. The all male group in summer suits, white shirts and thin ties, many with hats, crammed into the small hospital room. Large, noisy flash bulbs popped constantly. The reporters pushed and elbowed each other to make sure their questions were answered and that they got the best pictures.

Poor Dr. Popplewell, equally overwhelmed, stood in the corner of the room, helpless.

Connie lay nearly flat in her hospital bed, the head of the bed angled slightly upward. Her standard issue, wrinkled off-white hospital gown with a small blue print pattern and piping, open back, and no arms peeked from under the rumpled, bleached white sheet pulled halfway up her neck. Her right hand rested on her lower abdomen. Her right arm didn't move during the interview.

Her left arm bore a large, square white bandage on the outside of the elbow. Her hair was short and showed the effects of two days pressed into a pillow. Her right eye was swollen and had begun to show signs of bruising. Her face was swollen from the effects of the sleeping pills.

One of the newsmen asked if Connie wanted to tell her side of the story. As she began to speak, the reporters became quiet, straining to hear the halting, deliberate words of the Midwest's most famous alleged killer.

Connie started with a long, emotional narrative that riveted the room.

Connie Nicholas had been having an affair with Forrest Teel for fifteen years. During all of this time, Teel was married. In fact, during the course of their affair, Teel and his wife had adopted a son. She told of trips the two had taken to Havana, Cuba, to Chicago and St. Louis, each time registering in hotels as Mr. and Mrs. Forrest Teel. For the past three years, Teel paid her rent in her Marcy Lane apartment. In exchange, he had a key to her home and came and went as he pleased.

In Connie's mind, Forrest Teel was her one true love. He was the love, acceptance and security she had searched for her whole life. They would be married someday.

Three weeks ago, Connie had learned that Forrest Teel had a new girlfriend. Concerned, she began to follow him to see if it was true.

During the three weeks, Teel had seen her blue and white Chevrolet in the rearview mirror of his big Cadillac, stopped his car and confronted her. With a mixture of disgust and anger, he would tell her, "Connie, you've got to stop following me."

"He really raised hell with me for following him," she said.

She had discovered the phone number of Teel's new girlfriend and called it a couple of times. When the woman on the other end answered, Connie hung up without saying a word.

Connie and Teel had arguments about his relationship with the other woman. Understandably, Connie wanted him to give her up. Teel offered a unique, if not successful, explanation. He simply said that he was "sowing his oats" and that this new relationship would run its course. Then he would come back to Connie.

Connie reinforced her belief in his promise by pointing out that Teel had continued to date her even while dating the other woman. In fact, Connie and Teel had been out together each of the last two Saturdays that preceded the shooting. Connie sincerely believed that the new girl was no competition for her. Forrest Teel would come back to her. She believed that to the end.

Even after warnings from Teel, Connie continued to follow him. Finally, her detective work paid off. She watched his car park in front of an apartment in The Meadows and Teel get out and go in one of the doors.

After waiting an appropriate amount of time, she sneaked from her car along the front of the apartment building, dodging the windows as much as possible, past Teel's Cadillac and into the front entrance of the building. There were six apartments accessible from this entrance. Connie carefully made note of the last name listed for each apartment on the common mailbox.

She then compared the names to a directory of Lilly employees. One matched.

There was a secretary at Lilly named Laura Mowrer.

Connie continued. On the night of July 30, at 9:30, she drove her automobile to the Meadows Shopping Center. She now knew the apartment where Teel's new girlfriend lived. Sitting in the same space in the front of the apartment was the white Cadillac owned by Forrest Teel.

Connie drove about a quarter of a mile down the street, parked her car behind the Phillips 66 Station and walked back to the Cadillac. She checked the passenger door. It was unlocked. She climbed in and waited.

For three hours, she waited, alone in the darkness, watching the apartment through the front windshield of the car.

The curtains of Laura Mowrer's apartment were thin and unlined. Connie couldn't see any movement, but could clearly see that the lights were on when she arrived.

Later, the lights in the apartment went off, but Teel did not come out.

Then, a little before 1 AM, Teel emerged from the apartment. Unaware of the danger that awaited him, he approached the driver's side of the Cadillac, opened the door and climbed in. He was shocked and upset to find Connie Nicholas hiding crouched in the front passenger seat.

Immediately they began to argue. He started the car and backed from his parking space. She asked to go to her car. She directed him as he drove the one hundred or so yards.

He pulled in a parking space near her blue and white Chevy. "There's your car. Get out and go home," he said, staring straight ahead, fighting to contain his percolating anger.

The argument began again. According to Connie's account, the argument escalated. Then, according to Connie, Forrest Teel did something he had never done before.

He hit her.

Connie stopped her story to collect her thoughts.

"Did you shoot him?" came the first question from the reporters gathered in the room, their collective attention still focused on the woman in the bed.

"I think I shot him two or three times," she said, clutching the sheet in her left hand and pressing it to her neck.

He grabbed my right arm and threw me across the seat of the car." The gun in her right hand went off.

After a short silence, Connie went on. She hadn't meant to shoot, she said. She only bought the gun for protection on a trip she was planning to California.

Her tone suddenly changed. She became calm and very pensive.

She reminded the newsmen that Teel was the aggressor. He was the one who had hurt her. Implicitly, it was his own fault.

"I want you to make certain of one thing," she told them. "Be sure of this. I have a terribly black eye. My right arm is paralyzed. It feels like a piece of raw meat."

Somewhat melodramatically, she then began crying and screaming, "Why can't I move my arm? Why can't I move my arm?"

The reporters began asking specific questions.

"Did you regard Teel's new girlfriend as competition?"

She never once doubted that Teel would return to her, she replied.

"Did you feel let down when he found another girlfriend?

"No, no. He was coming back to me. He said it would all work itself out."

"Did he start the romance with you because he was let down by his wife?"

"No, no. He always loved me. In fact, he loved me five years before I loved him."

Connie had found the love for which she had searched for 35 years. And it was slipping away.

The tone of the press conference changed again. Connie realized that she was in control and that everyone was hanging on her every word. She began to make the most of it. Her natural charisma began to emerge. She liked feeling the acceptance of the crowd.

Yes, she was married when she started dating Teel.

She told a story of the time her second husband had actually walked in their home when Teel was there. She explained that Teel was a deliveryman bringing a case of Scotch. According to her, Curtis Nicholas bought the story.

She didn't get married to make Teel jealous. She was simply making a life for herself.

Teel was going to divorce his wife in 1961. There was no question about that. According to him, the Teels had already discussed it. They just wanted to wait until their son was out of high school.

She related how the two were never discreet, often going shopping together, being seen in public together often.

She had never met his wife, although she had seen her once in an ice skating rink.

"Will you try to commit suicide again?"

"I won't have the chance, unfortunately,"

"Do you know the other woman?"

"No, but I'd like to," she said with a wry, wicked smile.

"Why?"

She just rolled her head to the side and smiled.

At several points during the course of the interview, Connie broke into sobs, screaming that she didn't care what happened to her. Dr. Popplewell begged her to calm down.

As the conference was finally halted at the request of the doctor, Connie turned the tables on the reporters, asking them one final question.

"Can any of you recommend a lawyer? I'll need a good one."

In the back of the pack of reporters, one man looked different from the rest. He was dressed slightly different. The reason he was there was different.

Captain Michael Smiley had heard every word. And he didn't believe much of what he heard.

Now, he had to prove he was right.

When Laura Mowrer hit Indianapolis in 1955, she was the complete package. She was pretty, confident, outgoing when she wanted to be and well liked. But her attractive exterior and engaging personality hid the scars of her own less than perfect life.

Laura was born in Bridgeport, Illinois in 1929. Bridgeport began existence autonomously, but eventually ended up little more than a south-side suburb of Chicago.

The history of Bridgeport mirrored the development of Laura in that each had undergone several reincarnations, but survived each of several difficulties. In 1812, long before Bridgeport adopted its current name, the town was known simply as Lee's Place. This rather quaint name was a practical one. Among the first two American settlers in the area was Charles Lee, who arrived shortly after the establishment of Fort Dearborn in 1803. In April of 1812, for some unexplained reason, a group of ten to twelve Native American Indians, dressed in war paint and headdress, appeared unannounced at the Lee Farm. Visits from the Potawatamie Indians were not uncommon, however, these Indians did not look familiar and were quite imposing in their native war attire. After spending a rather tense day at the farm, the tenants unable to determine the intention of the Indians, but extending the guests every courtesy appropriate, two of the family members left by canoe. The Indians then proceeded to shoot, stab, mutilate and scalp the two remaining occupants. All of this was completed within earshot of the two fleeing family members.

The killing of 146 people by Indians sympathetic to the British during the War of 1812 just 4 months later put a virtual end to settlement of Lee's Place, Illinois.

By 1816, the land that would become Bridgeport would rise again, this time known as Hardscrabble.

Hardscrabble was a fitting name for the area. Most of the inhabitants were originally fur traders. However, as time passed, it became clear that a canal would be cut through the area and laborers began to apply for work on the project. In addition, a quarry was dug in 1833 to cut stone for an improvement project in the Chicago Harbor.

Although Hardscrabble was a descriptive name, ironically, the creations of the canal and the quarry marked the end of Hardscrabble. By 1833, the town has once again been renamed as Canal Port. Not until 1884 was there any mention of the town of Bridgeport.

But as the name Bridgeport took hold, various industries also took residence in the shadow of the rapidly expanding Chicago. Thanks mainly to the canal, meatpacking plants, lumberyards, grain elevators and several manufacturing plants sprung up. The commensurate number of saloons followed.

Laura's childhood corresponded with the peak period of growth in Bridgeport. But by the early 1950's, many companies began leaving the area, taking jobs with them. Trucks and trains replaced canal traffic and the industrial landscape reflected the shift.

Not long after high school was over, Laura had seen the handwriting on the wall.

A young man had caught young Laura's eye by the time she finished school. Like virtually all young men of the time, he was about to begin serving his time in the armed forces, in his case, the United States Navy. Unlike most young men, though, the Navy became his career. Laura could tolerate being a Navy wife for a short time. But the prospect of having an absentee husband while she was stuck in dying Bridgeport was too much for her.

Rather than ending with a bang, Laura's marriage ended with more of a whimper. The two became more and more distant, their interests diverged and, eventually, they just drifted their own separate ways. A good part of the time they were married was spent in Washington, D.C., where her husband was stationed. Laura eventually left Washington and her husband and secured a job at a battery factory near Evansville, Indiana, just across the Ohio River from Kentucky.

Dissatisfied with the life this position provided, in 1955, she arrived in Indianapolis to begin a job as a secretary at Eli Lilly and Company.

Laura's first housing was an apartment that she shared with another young lady. She made friends easily. But later, even her best friend and her roommate were shocked to discover that, not only had Laura been married before, she was still married when she came to Indianapolis. She was quietly divorced not long after arriving.

Shortly after arriving in Indianapolis, she joined a bridge club with several other young women at Lilly. It seemed everyone that knew Laura liked her.

Even now, her former coworkers describe her in glowing terms. "She was as cute as could be," said one.

The image of Laura was, for the most part, accurate. She was, indeed, a fun-loving, gregarious young woman with an infectious smile that can best be described as "impish." She was a good worker and was loyal to the men for whom she worked. In 1958, when her supervisor was transferred to another department, he made arrangements for Laura to be transferred with him.

Overall, Laura's life in Indianapolis was uneventful, for a while. She went out with friends, some nights staying out too late. She dated occasionally. She simply seemed to be an all-American, fun-loving girl.

But, like Forrest Teel, Laura was adept at showing only the side of her that she wanted others to see. Laura knew that information about certain things, like her marriage, would not help her in any way, so quite simply, she didn't give it out.

Laura had always been able to control the flow of information about herself to her friends and her coworkers. But on the Friday Morning of July 31, 1958, as she opened the door of her apartment in the Meadowbrook complex and picked up the morning paper, she felt her firm grasp slipping away. And with it, what everyone else would think of her.

Laura's new boyfriend had left her apartment less than six hours before. Now he was dead.

Laura's mind raced alternating between panic and anxiety. Should she run? Should she go to the police? What would she do when they found out about her?

One thing was certain in her mind. She couldn't face the people at work.

After cleaning out her desk at work in the early morning hours, Laura returned to her car. Once in her car, she drove around trying to figure out what to do. If she went to the police, they might think she killed him. News of Connie Nicholas had not yet been reported. But she struggled with the fact that she might have information that could help catch the killer. She began to think back to the night before.

Thursday night had been a regular date for Laura and Forrest Teel for almost three months now. She knew he was married, but she liked older men. Forrest Teel, an older man with money, power and good looks was too much for her to resist. Last night, Forrest had shown up at her door about 5:45 with Kosher food from a delicatessen they both liked. They ate dinner together, and spent the next several hours together.

At around 1:00 in the morning, he had left.

He always parked in the same space. It was a parking space that she could see from her living room window. She watched him walk from the door of the apartment building and open the car door of his new Cadillac. After getting in, he started the car and drove away, just as he had done every Thursday night in the weeks before.

She did remember that this time, though, he didn't blink his headlights as he pulled away. Although she thought that was odd, since he always made a point to say good-bye in this fashion, she honestly, didn't think too much about it.

Until now.

If only she had recognized that something was wrong. Had the killer been in the car, waiting for him? Was he trying to send her a signal?

Laura was caught squarely in a dilemma. She may be able to help catch the killer. And she may end her own life as she knew it.

In the end, Laura was true to the image that she carefully crafted for others to see. Laura sacrificed her personal reputation to help.

But she would do it on her terms, she decided.

By 9:00 AM, just hours after the killing, Laura had been in contact with her attorney, David Lewis. In slightly frantic tones, Laura explained her situation to Lewis and they agreed to meet later that morning.

Lewis was a well-known lawyer in Indianapolis and well respected, too. In the time before his meeting with Laura he did some research and devised a plan.

When the two met later that morning, Lewis outlined the plan. It basically involved two steps. First, they would get her to the police to tell her story. Second, they would get her out of town.

Laura agreed that Lewis' plan was the best she could hope for, given her unfortunate circumstances. She told him to go ahead.

Many times the police work long hours and days to locate witnesses. But every once in a while, witnesses find the police instead.

Once more, Captain Smiley found a lucky break on the other end of the phone line.

Attorney David Lewis was on the line. He said he had important information about the murder of Forrest Teel. Capt. Smiley immediately took the call.

Lewis identified himself, then informed Captain Smiley that he had been retained by a client that had some important information about the murder of Forrest Teel. Smiley made no mention of Connie Nicholas. As Lewis related the story of Teel's last night alive, Captain Smiley felt as though he had hit the jackpot.

Laura Mowrer wanted to talk; Laura Mowrer, for the last three months, the other woman in Forrest Teel's recently ended life.

Most everyone would agree that it took courage for Laura Mowrer to come forward. By this time, the case had already begun to capture widespread attention. The local newspapers were still reporting every detail of the crime, but, in addition, other media from around the country had begun reporting the story of the murder. This was going to be big, Laura knew, and there was no way she could get involved without inviting attention on herself. She knew that coming forward would subject her to unprecedented scrutiny.

She also knew that she would be branded for life.

Still, she made the difficult decision to contact the police and offer what she knew.

Smiley and Lewis arranged a secret meeting, outside of the glare of the press lights, later that same day. Laura was understandably nervous as Smiley interrogated the attractive young lady. Perhaps she would have been less nervous had she known that Connie Nicholas was already in custody, accused of the murder. However, Captain Smiley withheld that information for the time being.

Laura was very forthcoming with her information. She related every detail of their meetings and adulterous romance. Much of it would be very similar to the process Teel had used years before to seduce young Connie Nicholas. Laura was falling for the older man, but, luckily, hadn't fallen quite as far as Connie had—yet.

Within days of the murder of Forrest Teel, and her secret meeting with police, Laura Mowrer had left Indianapolis, fleeing to start a new life in San Bernardino, California. She doubted she would ever return to Indiana again.

Only two people knew where Laura had gone, Laura and her lawyer. The press started digging and found she had relatives in the Northeast. All of them assumed she had gone there. Again, Laura only showed what she wanted others to see. She simply let everyone involved believe she had gone east. In reality, she had gone the opposite direction. Truthfully, she might have liked to go Northeast. But, because of a strange and little known quirk in Indiana law at the time, a quirk that the public would not become aware of for several months, Laura couldn't go there.

At the same time Connie Nicholas was coming out of her comatose state and telling her side of the story, the newspapers were blaring from the headlines the identity of the "other woman."

By that time, Laura Mowrer was already gone.

Ironically, Forrest Teel had begun dating Connie Nicholas when she was 29, the same age as Laura.

Chapter 10

"Hope Rises Spurned Woman Will Recover—Teel's Last Love Also A Divorcee"
Page 1 Headline in the Indianapolis News
August 2, 1958

At her impromptu press conference, Connie had joked with reporters about the need for a lawyer, but she knew this was no joke. The seriousness of her situation had begun to settle on her and she knew she wouldn't be able to do this alone.

Even though she had been divorced two times before, each time she had simply agreed to use her husband's attorney. Both splits had been, for the most part, amicable, and she saw no need to secure her own lawyer. That would only cost her money, she thought.

But this time, she needed one herself. And, whether she knew it or not, she needed one fast.

By this time, the name Connie Nicholas was the most recognizable name in Indiana and much of the Midwest. She would quickly earn that same distinction around the country as well. Connie was smart enough to know that she couldn't just pick up the phone and start calling her old friends for the names of their family attorneys. So she asked her nurse for a phone book and looked up the number of the Indianapolis Bar Association.

She picked up the handset of the black rotary phone and dialed the number, a Melrose extension. In the days when phone numbers were a combination of words and numbers, Melrose extensions were in downtown Indianapolis. Virtually all of the lawyers were downtown.

The Indianapolis Bar Association maintained a lawyer referral service. While the attorneys in the referral service were categorized by "specialty," the fact was that most of the attorneys listed their names in several of the specialty categories. They wanted the best chance to get the most referrals. When a prospective client would call the Association and ask for an attorney to help with a probate matter, for example, the clerk would look in the probate category and refer the person to the next lawyer on the list. Many prospective clients believed they were being referred to the best attorney for their case. However, in reality, they would simply receive the next name on the list.

It was truly the luck of the draw for both the attorney and the prospective client.

Luckily for Connie Nicholas, the person on the other end of the phone didn't ask for a name. He simply gave the polite caller the names of the first three attorneys on his list who checked "criminal law" on the form they filled out when they registered with the referral service.

Connie picked up the phone and called the first name, Charles Symmes.

It was the best call she could have made.

In 1958, Charlie Symmes was what many termed a renaissance lawyer. Although he was a competent criminal defense lawyer, the truth was, like many attorneys then and now, he made his money on virtually anything that walked in the door. But Charlie was different. Charlie Symmes possessed a deep knowledge of many facets of the law.

Many lawyers who are in the "general practice" of law end up as the proverbial jacks of all trades, masters of none. They become quite proficient at simple cases, but are lost on any with depth and complexity.

But Charlie had an innate ability to handle complex cases in many different areas. Indeed, he could handle complicated cases in different areas at the same time. It was not uncommon for Symmes to go from a discussion of criminal law to the law of estates or corporations with ease.

So well respected was Charlie Symmes for his knowledge of criminal law, among other topics, that the publisher of the leading treatise for lawyers on criminal law in Indiana entrusted the preparation of the annual supplement to him for thirty years.

Legal organizations also tapped Symmes as a lecturer at seminars for other lawyers of topics as diverse as wills, estates and domestic relations.

The 40 year-old Symmes was very small, maybe 5' 6". He may have weighed 120 pounds after a large meal. Charlie was health conscious his entire life, but was also blessed with hereditary traits that kept him quite thin. Like all professional men of the day, he wore his slightly receding hair short, slicked and combed to the side. His round, light tortoiseshell glasses gave him a very appropriate "studious" look.

Symmes' appearance made him very easy to underestimate. Those that made that mistake did not do so a second time.

The diminutive Symmes had a solid reputation in the community at the time. However, he had never handled a case of this magnitude before. Of course, no one in Indianapolis had before.

But to say that Connie Nicholas was lucky in this draw was an understatement.

Later that same day, Symmes rushed over and visited Connie Nicholas in General Hospital. They talked for about an hour, but he made no commitments to the notorious defendant. This would be the biggest case of his career and he was smart enough to make sure he could handle it.

One thing that marks a good lawyer is that he knows when he needs expertise from others. And Charlie was definitely a good lawyer.

Symmes knew he needed help. Before accepting the case, he consulted one of the top criminal defense lawyers in Indianapolis in the 1950's. Charlie's goal was not simply to collect advice. It was to convince the other lawyer to join him in representing the most famous defendant in Indiana and the U.S.

The man was undisputedly the top criminal defense lawyer in Indiana at the time. He had been a criminal court judge and had handled several high profile cases in the past few years. All told, he had fifty years in the practice of criminal law. And while most lawyers of his vintage were retiring, at 76, this one was still making his mark. Truthfully though, Charlie Symmes had an "in" with this attorney.

Symmes was almost certain he could convince him to help. After all, he had known the other lawyer his entire life.

Charlie needed the best criminal defense lawyer around. So he called his dad.

Within hours, Charlie was representing Connie Nicholas. And with Charlie's dad, Frank's, help, Connie Nicholas was going to get one of the best defenses possible.

Charlie and Frank immediately announced to the press that they would be representing this most well-known of defendants. The circus atmosphere that was developing around the case tempted them to talk to the reporters. They had the opportunity to say the right things and be literally on the front page of every paper in the country. Unlike many of today's lawyers, the thought never crossed either of their minds.

"No comment," was all they would say.

Together, by their own experiences, Charlie and Frank knew how to try a case. And they were not planning to do anything different on this one.

The two-man defense team had a tremendous job ahead of it. And they knew it. Technically, with their experience, they could handle the defense. However, they discussed the possibility of bringing on another attorney to help with the load. They discussed the best candidate for the job and agreed on an up-and-coming young lawyer. When they made the phone call, Joe Quill jumped at the chance. This would be his biggest case, would potentially make him a household name and give him the opportunity to learn from two of the best lawyers in Indiana.

Now that the defense team was complete, it certainly had its work cut out for it. Connie Nicholas hadn't done herself any favors in her defense so far. She had the motive, she had the weapon in her possession when she was arrested. The fact she had attempted suicide indicated her guilt. But all that paled by the fact that she had already admitted her guilt to the police. And, worse, yet, she had also admitted it to the press!

Trying a case to a judge, without a jury, is called a bench trial. The veteran defense lawyers knew that they had no chance in a bench trial. The judge would hear the evidence, apply the law and convict Connie of first-degree murder, a conviction that would make her eligible to die in the electric chair. The judge would, perhaps rightfully, exclude all evidence of her relationship with the victim and psychological state at the time in rendering his judgment. Even if the judge bought Connie's story that the shooting was an accident, he would surely convict her of manslaughter. Trying the case to the judge, without a jury, is the defendant's choice. But the defense team knew her chance of leaving the courtroom without handcuffs after a trial to the judge was nonexistent.

The only chance she would have at beating a murder charge was a jury trial. But in a case such as this, everyone in Indianapolis had already heard all of the savory details through newspaper accounts. The chances of finding a sympathetic jury comprised of people that hadn't yet formed an opinion about Connie's guilt were slim and none.

Neither alternative looked especially promising.

All three of the defense lawyers were feeling the stress. Murder cases are always stressful. After all, a person's liberty, and maybe even life, are at stake. Plus, this was the largest case of their individual careers and, literally, the world would be watching.

The next step was damage control.

Even though the defense team had originally had no comment, they soon realized that the people that were reading the stories in the newspapers about their client were the same ones that would be judging her in a court of law in a few short months. Together they revised their strategy. From that point forward, the lawyers would not seek publicity for their client. That was not their style and they found that repulsive and undignified. Good attorneys don't do that type of thing, they believed.

However, when any one of them was asked about the case, going to or coming from court, they would say that they are confident that she will be acquitted. The idea was to introduce some potential doubt into the minds of the jurors even before they are called for jury duty, even if in reality, they didn't have any proof that she didn't do it.

Expectations were high for the new prosecutor Phil Bayt. After serving as controller and mayor, the public had expectations of him that were, in all probability, greater than his abilities. Much like Judge Tom Faulconer, he had never handled a murder trial before in any capacity. The new prosecutor would need a conviction. Not yet even in office, Bayt called on two of his most talented deputies to handle the case. Bayt would attend the trial and help as he could. But the ball would be carried by his two deputies.

Francis Thomason was about 5' 10" tall with wavy black hair cut close on the sides. His face was wrinkled and his eyes had natural bags underneath. He was in his late 50s. The veteran prosecuting attorney knew his way around the Marion County Courts. He had earned his job as chief deputy prosecuting attorney.

Where Francis Thomason brought experience, deputy prosecutor Judson Hagerty brought youth and energy to the prosecution team. The handsome young redhead had movie star looks. Every day, he wore a dapper suit, white shirt and a white handkerchief neatly folded and tucked in the breast pocket of his jacket. Jud never had a hair out of place. But he was more than good looking. He was confident, but not cocky. Sure of himself without being overbearing. And he had no reservations about sparring with attorneys bearing much more experience than he.

The team complemented each other well. Thomason was the veteran. He had made the prosecutor's office his career. Haggerty was the youngster. He was there for the experience. Then he would go into private practice. Thomason was cerebral. Haggerty was fiery. The differences could have been troublesome. But each knew the other's strength and respected the differences. The Symmes-led defense team was in for a challenge.

By now, Judge Saul Rabb was a lame duck. Having lost the election in November, 1958, he was counting down the days before he would be forced to relinquish the bench of which he had been the sole occupant since its creation in 1947. But he had some unfinished business to take care of first.

Rabb knew that the Connie Nicholas trial was going to be big. He also knew that the publicity could be very extensive and beneficial for the presiding judge. Since he would be in need of a job soon, he recognized the potential exposure the trial would bring.

So Judge Rabb set his sights on a trial for Connie Nicholas November 24, 1958, just weeks before his term would end.

Of course the veteran judge knew that he would have to hurry things along to get a trial started that quickly. But he desperately wanted to try this case.

With luck, the murder trial of Connie Nicholas would be Judge Saul Rabb's finale.

Two outstanding issues had to be resolved before the trial could start. The defense filed a motion asking the court to suppress all of the evidence found in Connie's apartment the day after the murder. They argued that the police had no right to enter the apartment without a search warrant. Because of the quick pace of events at the time, no search warrant was requested. Therefore, none was issued.

The defense argument was a good one. After all, no one was in the apartment, there was no danger or imminent threat to the officers or others. Yet they still entered the apartment. Even if the officers entered the apartment in good faith, the father-son team argued, once they entered and discovered that no one was present, they should have left without disturbing anything.

The prosecutors countered that the officers did not have the benefit of hindsight. When they entered the apartment they had no knowledge that no one was inside. It was plausible to the officers that Connie could have been inside dying. She had left a suicide note, after all. And, once inside, the police only looked at things that were in plain view. The circumstances had to be looked at from the police point of view at the time, they maintained.

Quickly after arguments, the Judge ruled that the evidence was admissible and that no search warrant was required.

Unfortunately for Judge Rabb, the second issue would not be resolved as easily.

Connie had been in the hospital now since being found near death on July 31. By the end of November, she had not left the building in over four months. While she was making progress and had fully recovered from her attempted drug overdose, she was still having difficulty with her arm and hand. Indeed, upon being found, she had complained about her right hand. Now she complained of pain and problems with her left.

As the November trial date approached, it became more and more clear that Connie Nicholas would be in no shape to stand trial. The defense team petitioned Judge Rabb for a continuance and, since the defendant has a constitutional right to attend the trial, he had little choice but to grant the motion.

Reluctantly, Judge Rabb had to admit that he would not try Connie Nicholas.

The Indianapolis Star on November 5, 1958 carried the election results in a table format that filled almost half the page. Faulconer had won the Criminal Court #2 bench by 5,600 votes. Next to the election returns was a one-column article with the headline, "Nicholas Trial is Continued." The story went on to explain that the extended hospital stay had caused Judge Rabb to issue an order continuing the trial indefinitely.

The new judge in Criminal Court #2 would set the trial date when he took office.

Along with the transfer of the gavel for Criminal Court #2, came the stress. Judge Saul Rabb's stress of trying to get the Connie Nicholas trial in before he left the bench was disappointingly eased in January, 1958. Judge Faulconer's was just beginning.

Physically, Faulconer, by this time, was looking more the part of judge than he had in his first election attempt. His fondness of Milky Way Candy Bars and butterscotch Dairy Queen milkshakes had helped his weight to a hefty 230 pounds. Never one to exercise absent a doctor's order, he carried quite a bit of the weight in his midsection and face. The press routinely described him as portly.

The wire-rimmed glasses he had worn as a young lawyer were now replaced by thick, black horn-rimmed frames, a style he would keep for many years to come. His hair had thinned and the slight redness had faded into blonde.

While, certainly, Judge Thomas J. Faulconer, III was feeling the stress as did Judge Raab, his was for a completely different reason. There is a common misconception among non-lawyers that law school teaches lawyers to be lawyers. But Faulconer knew well that this isn't quite true. Law school teaches students to think like lawyers. The surprising fact is that most all lawyers complete law school without ever stepping in a courtroom. And although Faulconer had been in his share of courtrooms by now, he knew that he had never experienced what was about to be brought upon him.

In the midst of learning the procedures in his new court, meeting new people and uprooting most of the stability in his life, Faulconer would have to prepare for the biggest moment in his life. At the same time, he would have to find time for his wife and three young daughters.

How life had changed in a few short years.

To add to the stress, a recurring thought pervaded the new Judge's mind. He had never presided over a murder trial. He had never prosecuted a murder trial. He had never defended anyone accused of murder. He hadn't appeared as a witness in a murder trial.

He had never even seen a murder trial.

There is a saying among lawyers that a good lawyer pays a judge's salary in taxes each year. For many top lawyers, that is very true and, in some cases, a substantial understatement. Plus, in many respects, the judge's job is much harder. A lawyer can pick and choose his cases, rejecting those he finds distasteful or even simply difficult. A judge loses the luxury of that choice when he ascends to the bench.

Judge Faulconer had no choice but to reluctantly face the task he had worked so hard to obtain.

And so, Judge Faulconer began studying. From the day he found out he was to be the judge on Indiana's biggest case, through the day he was sworn in, he studied. Those interested in the case had no idea that the judge was so inexperienced that he began his studies by studying the procedures for simply calling a jury. But as time progressed, like a general readying himself for battle, Judge

Faulconer laid out his plan. He would begin by reviewing all documents that had been filed in the case. Immediately upon being sworn, he would begin a careful and thorough examination of the file.

In addition, he would begin preparing the case as if he were a lawyer on the case. He would begin by preparing the prosecution's case, then prepare the defendant's case. By placing himself in the shoes of each party, he hoped to anticipate the issues and objections that would be raised during the trial.

Judges have three sources upon which they can rely to make decisions. First, they can rely on code books, books that contain the mountains of legislation at the federal, state and local levels. Second, when no direct statute or ordinance can be found, judges look for similar cases. These similar cases, known as precedent, can at least give the judge insight into another judge's thought pattern when faced with a similar situation. At best, the right case can tell the judge exactly how to decide the issue. At least, a similar case can help the judge's thought process in his decision. The third situation is the most stressful. When a judge cannot locate an applicable law and cannot find any similar cases, put simply, he must make the law himself. The judge has no other choice. Since he can't simply refuse to decide, he must issue a ruling. That ruling then becomes the law in that area or jurisdiction that others must follow.

With each day of preparing, Judge Faulconer was more determined to minimize the surprises in the trial of Connie Nicholas.

He researched proper procedure for criminal cases, learned how to call a jury, something he had never done before, and poured over any pertinent information that he could find. He talked to friends and fellow lawyers. He poured over lawbooks researching proper procedure and voraciously reading cases that bore the slightest resemblance to the situations he might encounter in the coming weeks. He was determined that he would have a fair and efficient trial.

Eventually, his vast research would be compiled into a three ring binder, his trial notebook. He spent hours filling it, then additional hours organizing and familiarizing himself with it. He ran hypothetical situations through his head and consulted his notebook to attempt to resolve them. He also made a mental list of people he could consult if he needed help.

Unfortunately, the one person that Faulconer had relied on throughout the last eight years for guidance and support could not offer any in this case. With Phil Bayt as one of the prosecutors of Connie Nicholas, Faulconer would now be the decision-maker rather than the student.

The roles were reversed.

It seemed Faulconer's life had come full circle in less than a decade. The one-time fresh, inexperienced lawyer who was trolling the town for a part-time job to pay the bills when he stumbled into the man who would be mayor, was now the judge, making the decisions that would control the lives of the defendant, as well as his mentor.

The stress on the young judge was enormous.

The judge's trial notebook grew to several inches thick. The brown vinyl binder was never far from his side. He took it to work, he took it home. He reviewed it and added to it every day.

Unfortunately, no amount of preparation prepared Faulconer for the first decision he would have to make in the case of the State of Indiana vs. Connie Nicholas. His first decision would be a difficult one, and it would be made even before the trial started. In a real sense, it had nothing to do with the guilt or innocence of Connie Nicholas in the murder of Forrest Teel.

Instead, it had to do with the American Bar Association.

The American Bar Association is a quasi-governing agency for lawyers in the United States. While membership in the Bar Association is not mandatory, the majority of lawyers do belong. So did Judge Faulconer.

Although the only binding rules on judges come from the state and federal government, the Bar Association has considerable power due to its large and influential membership. The rules that the Bar Association promulgates are usually accepted as gospel, whether a legislature or other governing body actually enacts them or not. To go against the Bar Association was similar to crossing one's brethren. And yet, that was just the decision that faced the freshman judge.

As the time for the Connie Nicholas trial approached, the young judge found himself on the receiving end of repeated requests to allow what promised to be a sensational trial broadcast on television. No trial in the United States had ever been broadcast live in 1958. Indeed, with a very, very few exceptions, no motion picture cameras had ever been allowed in a U.S. courtroom. The most notable exception recently had been the Sam Shepherd case in Ohio, the case that gave rise to the fictional television series "The Fugitive."

The reason for this was quite simple.

Since its inception in 1878, the American Bar Association membership has charged itself with maintaining the ethical standards of the legal profession. These rules had undergone several revisions in that time, both major and minor and continue to be revised today.

In 1958, the rules governing the conduct of lawyers were organized into individual topics called Canons. Canon 35 was quite simple and straightforward. No cameras were allowed in courtrooms.

According to the reasoning of the Bar Association, cameras in a courtroom would have a devastating and prejudicial effect on the proceedings. Witnesses would potentially embellish stories to make the newspapers. People would become nervous and play to the cameras.

The proceedings would turn into the proverbial circus, the Association warned.

Most every judge in the country at that time simply abided by Canon 35 without question. But most judges were not under the pressure from the press to allow cameras that Judge Faulconer was under. Most court proceedings were not likely to be televised even if the opportunity was presented. The interest simply wasn't there.

The law is not stagnant. It can't be. It will adapt to changing circumstances over time. However, its reaction time is painfully slow. Before simply accepting Canon 35 as a given, Faulconer made a bold decision for a 35 year-old judge with less than 90 days on the bench.

He decided to consider the possibility of cameras in the Connie Nicholas trial.

Canon 35 had been in effect for many years. It had been adopted by the Association without much fanfare. But it had been adopted in a different time by different men. It was adopted in a time when motion picture cameras were a novelty and quite rare and still cameras were larger, noisier and substantially more intrusive. But by the 1950's motion picture films were becoming a major source of entertainment in American homes, and, a source for information. Every city of appreciable size had at least one television station now and national networks were the mainstay of weekly programming.

The times had changed, and Judge Faulconer knew it.

But the decision was still difficult. First, to allow cameras in the courtroom was to clearly express his rejection of one of the principle tenets of the organization that governed his craft. The political implications for a new judge with further political aspirations could be enormous. He knew the safe road was to cite Canon 35 and decline the requests for coverage of the trial.

Plus, the young lawyer was concerned about his reputation. One wrong choice on an issue this big and he would forever be known as one who couldn't follow the rules, a dangerous distinction for an aspiring judge and politician in 1959.

Maybe most importantly, Judge Faulconer had never even tried a jury trial or a murder trial. To allow media coverage could also mean broadcast of any mistakes or miscues on his part.

The real fact is that a sitting judge can do pretty much whatever he wants in his courtroom, absent some criminal conduct. The rebuke may come when an appellate court overturns his actions and he has to possibly retry the case, ever mindful of the slap on the wrist from the higher court. So regardless of the decision that Faulconer made, it would happen the way he decided - at least in the short term.

The thing he was most scared of though, was that if Connie Nicholas was convicted, she would appeal the case based on the media coverage, the appellate court would reverse the conviction and Faulconer would have to try the case from beginning to end again.

Not to mention that the whole world would know that Faulconer had been wrong.

The young judge struggled with the dilemma he faced. The easy way out, honoring the Association's Canon, was tempting. But he had a nagging feeling that, if handled correctly, the case could be covered by cameras and still result in a fair trial.

In reality, Faulconer was not the first to struggle with this issue. Earlier that same year, several public officials in Indianapolis had been tried in connection with a scandal involving the building of public highways. The outcry for press coverage of those trials was also heard, although on a more local level. Ironically, the courtroom in which the highway scandal trials had taken place was, coincidentally, Marion County Criminal Court #2. Judge Saul Rabb had faced the same dilemma in the same courtroom mere months before.

Rabb had eventually made the decision to allow the cameras. However, he set no limitations on the photographers. Consequently, the circus atmosphere prophesied by the American Bar Association had materialized. Photographers would approach the witness stand during testimony, getting tight shots of the witnesses with flash bulbs that illuminated a city block. To say the press had affected the witnesses was a grand understatement.

One of the many interested spectators in the courtroom during portions of the highway scandal trials was a young lawyer named Thomas Faulconer. Reflecting on that experience just a few months later, he knew he could not let the Connie Nicholas trial be run the same way.

The public knew little of the struggle between the old line Bar Association and the media. The television stations monitored and lobbied the judge daily, hoping for a decision in their favor.

Before making a decision on the media presence, Faulconer set a trial date for jury selection in the Connie Nicholas trial. It would start on March 16, 1959. In January, due to the exceptional publicity, the judge would order jury summonses be sent to 200 registered voters in Marion County, four times the usual call of 50.

He would quickly find that even he had underestimated the pervasive curiosity into the murder of Forrest Teel.

One evening, before going home, Judge Faulconer sat on the bench in Criminal Court #2 and surveyed the room where the future of Connie Nicholas would be decided. The round, heavyset 35 year-old leaned forward in his red leather, high back swivel chair, his elbows on the bench in front of him, his hands combing through his thin, reddish-blonde hair. Even though it was one floor beneath the grandeur of Criminal Court #1 in a half-basement much like the first level in a tri-level house, it might as well have been on another continent. No polished woods, no balcony, no marble. The tiny courtroom had been an afterthought when the court was created in 1947 and it showed.

Much of the judge's bench was just stained plywood. Exposed pipes painted the colors of the walls, dark brown on the bottom and cream on the top, ran from floor to ceiling on almost every wall. Large electric pedestal fans stood in two opposite corners. The room would accommodate but 68 spectators in three rows of hard, wooden chairs. A tarnishing, tubular brass rail separated the counsel tables from the spectators, but by merely two or three feet. The only padded chairs in the room belonged to the judge and the jury which would be seated to Judge Faulconer's left.

The floor was a checkerboard of black and white tiles throughout. Six long windows let sunlight in, each running from about waist height to the tall ceiling 12 feet up. Horizontal blinds covered the wire mesh in the windows. A large paper calendar for 1959 hung tacked to one wall, a gift from the State Automobile Insurance Association. The circulation of air from the fans sometimes caused it to hang slightly crooked.

The judge wondered to himself what he had gotten himself into.

How does a newly-elected judge at the tender age of 35 prepare for, not only his first murder trial, but the first jury trial of his career? Add to this his growing awareness as the trial date approached that his every word and action would be reported and scrutinized by not only the local print, TV and radio, but also the news media from throughout the country. And, it appeared quite possibly, the world.

This was a fundamental struggle for the young man. He had developed a strong belief that the public had the right to know what went on in government. To keep the press out would fly in the face of his strong conviction in favor of this right. However, logistically and politically, he wondered how he could possibly let the television, newspapers and radio in.

He couldn't let it turn into the fiasco of the highway scandal trials the year before.

As he reflected on the increasing inquiries from the local, out of state and national press, the young man grew more and more concerned that his fragile judicial reputation and future political career would be determined by how he conducted this, his first murder trial, his first jury trial.

He then got up and went home.

In February, 1959, as Judge Faulconer prepared for the trial of his life, and Connie Nicholas lay in General Hospital, two moving trucks rolled north on Washington Boulevard. They were an odd sight as trucks were not allowed on boulevards in Indianapolis except for local deliveries. In this case, rather than a delivery, the trucks were making a pickup.

Faced with the prospect of maintaining the large house that was but one icon of her deceased husband's success, Mary Elizabeth Teel sold the house on Washington Boulevard and moved herself, her possessions and her son to a much smaller home about a mile west. Although Tommy would attend a different high school, he could still maintain his friendships during this difficult time in the lives of both remaining Teels.

The house was only two bedrooms, but was very well-appointed. It had a price tag of $40,000, still well above the price for a home attainable by most in Indianapolis. Indeed the Crow's Nest neighborhood was a quiet hideaway favored by some of Indianapolis' old money of the day.

Moving from the house seemed to offer Mrs. Teel the opportunity to shed herself of the last mementos of her troubled life with Forrest. Unfortunately, she would find that her troubles would follow her to her new home as well.

In the meantime, as the March 16 trial date approached, Connie Nicholas received word from her doctors that she was finally well enough to leave the hospital. Most patients who had been in the hospital for such an extended period of time and had undergone two major surgeries on their hands would be overjoyed. But most of them would not be leaving the hospital for a jail cell.

On Friday, March 13, authorities at General Hospital notified Sheriff Robert O'Neal that Mrs. Nicholas' treatment for injuries to her hand could continue on an outpatient basis. She would no longer need to remain in the hospital's prison ward.

The letter received by Sheriff O'Neal requested that the defendant be returned to the hospital each evening after court to continue her therapy. After receiving physical therapy, she would be returned to the jail each night.

"This is a surprise to us," Charlie Symmes said after being notified by the press. "It was our understanding she would remain in custody at the hospital during the trial."

With the pressure on Connie of the looming trial would be added a move to the Marion County Jail.

Just days before the trial for her life would begin, Connie Nicholas first set foot in prison. She was assigned to an empty cell, vacated hours before by a shoplifter who had served her sentence.

In spite of the efforts of Dr. Martin Luther King, Jr. and Thurgood Marshall, among others, the women's prisons and jails were still segregated in Indiana in 1959. Connie was the only occupant of her cell which could accommodate two. However, she was one of eight female prisoners in that part of the Marion County Jail. Black women prisoners stayed in another facility. Connie quickly became fast friends with her fellow inmates. Indeed, one had been briefly confined to the prison ward of General Hospital, so the two were already acquainted. She, too, was in for murder, although as an accessory.

The women took to Connie quickly. No makeup was allowed and the women all wore the same pale green prison issue dress. Still, the other women immediately began offering Connie help in getting dressed and combing her hair as she struggled to regain the use of her arms and hands.

By this time, the doctors had told Connie that she may never regain full use of her fingers, due to the extensive nerve damage. The cause of the nerve damage would be a central issue in the upcoming trial. Connie maintained that it was primarily the result of the struggle for the gun in the Cadillac. The prosecution claimed it was either caused by her position in the car, her head resting atop her hand for hours, or just an act altogether.

The doctors had fashioned very elaborate braces for both arms made of aluminum rods, padding and rubber bands. In retrospect, they have the appearance of archaic torture devices. According to Connie, they were quite painful and were as cumbersome as they appeared. Connie could only tolerate them for short periods and the other women helped her put them on and take them off.

Her first weekend in prison was more tolerable than she had expected. However, she still didn't sleep well. The prison didn't have pillows. And she was just hours away from her trial for murder.

The weekend papers ran stories of the cost of Connie's hospital stay to taxpayers. Her nearly 8 months in the hospital, including three surgeries, had cost the taxpayers of Indianapolis $5,148. That included $85.00 in surgical fees and $10.00 for the recovery room.

Connie had spent eight months in the solitude of the hospital. However, this time was not wasted. Primarily she had three policemen assigned to guard her and her room during that time. She became friendly with each of them, often telling her side of the story in an attempt to gain their sympathy. At least one of the guards wasn't buying it. But immediately upon her transfer to the jail, Patrolman George Johnson, who was one of Connie's three principal guards during her stay at General Hospital, told the assembling press, "I believe she is innocent."

Apparently fearing retribution for his statement, Patrolman Johnson refused to provide his first name or any other personal details in his statements to the press. Within hours, however, his name and background were uncovered and accompanied many of the stories of his opinion.

"If Connie says her gun went off in a struggle—and she's told me all about it - then that's the way it happened," he had said"

The streetwise veteran personally vouched for the veracity and loyalty of the defendant. "She wouldn't run, anyway. I just know if she were left unguarded, she wouldn't run. She's not that kind of person."

In three days, she would have to convince the jury of the same thing. And more.

As expected, Patrolman Johnson would be publicly reprimanded and censured by the police chief for his remarks.

Chapter 11

"Trial to Bare Connie's Life, Love for Teel"
Page 1 Headline of the Indianapolis Times
March 15, 1959

The term "courtroom drama" is one of life's true oxymorons. Even in the most sensational of cases, the great majority of testimony and discussion in the courtroom is quite technical and extremely boring. Still, the American public has a fascination with what goes on in the marbled halls of justice. So when the Connie Nicholas trial was scheduled to begin on March 16, hopeful spectators turned out in droves.

On an uncharacteristically cold Spring day when the high temperature didn't even reach freezing, literally hundreds of people lined the dirty interior basement hallway hoping to get one of the coveted seats inside Criminal Court #2. The tiny courtroom only held fifty or so spectators after a slight reconfiguration of the room to accommodate the spectacular jury trial. Judge Faulconer had already declared that standing would not be allowed by spectators.

Those that donned their winter coats, hats and gloves and rode the buses and drove their cars downtown that day were disappointed. With the size of the courtroom and the number of potential jurors called for the trial, the courtroom was full before any spectators were admitted. Aside from attorneys, court personnel and the prospective jurors, Judge Faulconer did order three seats set aside on the front row. Connie's sister, brother and sister-in-law would attend daily. Still, the faithful remained in the warm, if not particularly comfortable hallway anxiously awaiting updates on the trial's progress. Still others gathered at the windows of the courtroom, taking turns pressing their face against the foggy glass to see the most infamous criminal of the late 1950s.

Besides possibly glimpsing Connie Nicholas in the flesh, dressed in a gray and black wool suit with a matching hat, these history seekers saw little else that Monday. Jury selection would be much more difficult and time consuming than even the attorneys and judge expected.

The trial began with the announcement of Judge Faulconer's first decision. He would allow press coverage of the trial. A media area would be roped off to his right. But each member of the press would have to agree to abide by certain rules.

During the prelude to jury selection, Judge Faulconer continued to wrestle with his pending decision to allow cameras in the courtroom. As he had at other times in his life, and as he would continue to do during the coming trial, the judge sought out someone with more practical experience in dealing with the issue at hand. In the late 1950s, one of the more prominent newsmen was an anchorman on WFBM-TV named Ken Myers. Judge Faulconer called him and asked for his help.

Ken Myers was a handsome man at the top of his career. He was the main anchorman on the one and only television station in Indianapolis. He looked to be around 40 years old, yet was already a trusted face and voice in the living rooms of thousands in central Indiana.

By now, Judge Faulconer had all but made up his mind that he was going to go against Canon 35 of the American Bar Association and allow cameras into the courtroom during the Connie Nicholas trial. But the logistics of such a decision were intimidating. As he conferred with Ken Myers, the judge insisted that he could only allow the cameras if rules and controls were put in place that would prevent disruption. Having the benefit of hindsight in the highway scandal trials in his own courtroom, Faulconer knew his reputation would suffer immeasurably if his decision to allow cameras turned out to be the wrong one.

Ken Myers and Judge Faulconer worked together to formulate a few basic rules designed to allow the judge to rule the courtroom rather than the press and photographers. In the days leading up to the trial, Judge Faulconer conferred on occasion with Ken Myers, fine-tuning these rules and talking out possible scenarios.

By the first day of trial, Judge Faulconer was comfortable with the rules they had promulgated.

First, noisy cameras would not be allowed. If the judge heard anything beyond a low hum, he would order the camera shut off and the operator out of the courtroom.

Second, while court was in session, there would be no pictures of the jury. The jurors were not on trial, he said.

Third, any photograph of a witness must include the court reporter. Judge Faulconer did not want photographers getting too close to the witnesses.

Fourth, Judge Faulconer ordered that no additional microphones be used. In 1959, the technology of the day was such that microphones had to be placed in front of the witnesses to clearly pick up testimony. Additionally, each media source would have to have its own microphone. Faulconer did not want a mass of twenty or thirty microphones facing the witnesses. Consequently, there was virtually no audio track on the footage shown on television.

Finally, live television was not allowed. Proceedings could be filmed and aired later. Upon learning of his ruling allowing media coverage, several members of the press had asked the judge, obviously friendly to the media, if the trial could be broadcast live on television. The judge polled the attorneys involved along with the defendant and, as all were opposed, rejected the request. However, two radio stations were allowed to broadcast the trial live in its entirety.

Despite the restraints, the media were ecstatic.

For all of the judge's preparation and study, he was still understandably nervous. This would be the first jury trial of his life and would probably be the biggest. He wanted to do everything within his power to avoid making a mistake that would cause a reversal by an appellate court later. More than that, he wanted to make sure he didn't do anything embarrassing.

When he left his pale green, wood-sided Cape Cod house for court on March 16, he alerted his wife to his game plan. Whenever an issue would arise about which there was any doubt, he would be calling a recess, retreating to his chambers, consulting his meticulously prepared notebook, and finding the right answer before making a ruling.

"The press may say I am the dumbest judge that ever sat on the bench, but I have to do this right."

He followed his game plan throughout.

Jury selection is an art. And a competent trial lawyer knows that picking a favorable jury will make proving his case much easier. But the process is slow and tedious, to say the least.

In truth, a good lawyer will actually begin trying his case during the jury selection process. By asking questions that include a few of the facts that will be introduced during the trial, an attorney can gauge the reaction of the prospective juror even before deciding to accept him for the panel. The Nicholas defense team began meeting in Symmes' office in the 10 story Lemke Building one block east of the courthouse in downtown Indianapolis.

The first step in jury selection is to dismiss any potential jurors that would automatically be disqualified anyway. In 1959 Indiana, anyone over age 65 did not have to serve. Those wanting to leave were excused.

The jury selection process affords each side the opportunity to question the beliefs, morals and tendencies of the remaining panel. Since the goal of jury selection for each side is to get a jury that will be favorable to it, the attorneys ask questions that are likely to predict the manner in which a juror is likely to vote.

Each side may "strike" as many jurors as it desires so long as there is a reason, or "cause." The judge decides whether cause exists. For example, if a potential juror is related to a witness or knows the defendant, the judge will likely find the juror is dismissed for cause.

In addition, each side is allotted a number of "peremptory" strikes. These strikes may be used for any reason whatsoever. No rationale is required to strike a potential juror using a peremptory strike.

In typical criminal cases, each side is given an unlimited number of strikes for cause and three to five peremptory strikes. Because of the pervasive publicity of the Connie Nicholas trial, each side was given 20 peremptory strikes in addition to the unlimited strikes for cause.

Effective use of strikes is essential. So each side met in the days leading up to jury selection to plot their respective strategies for using their strikes to seat the best jury possible.

The jury selection process today bears little resemblance to the same process that existed in the 1950s. Today, jurors are given a questionnaire that is reviewed by the judge. Any answer that indicates prejudice results in dismissal even prior to the attorney's questions. Today, judges are allowed, and even encouraged, to question the jurors to determine the fitness of each for service on the jury.

In the 1950's, the judge played a much different role. His function was that of referee. All questions were asked by the attorneys. The judge's only real function in the process was to rule on questions of strikes for cause. Only as a part of that ruling was he allowed to question the potential jurors.

After the summary dismissal of potential jurors who qualified for voluntary removal, the attorneys for each side began the questioning. The questions posed to each of the remaining prospective jurors were consistent. Each question was designed to cull the undesirable jurors and to plant the basic theories of the case in the minds of the remaining jurors.

Charlie Symmes conducted the questioning for the defense.

"Do you think a defendant has to prove her innocence?"

"Should a defendant have to testify in her behalf?"

"Do you think a person has the right to defend himself if he is assaulted?

"Would the fact that a person attempted to commit suicide prejudice you against her?"

"Would the fact that a person had an affair make you prejudiced?"

"Would you be prejudiced if the evidence showed that the defendant owned a gun?"

"If the evidence showed that the defendant had been divorced twice, would that prejudice you?"

Jud Haggerty countered with questions such as, "What do you think about the death penalty?"

"Do you realize that the law says human life is regarded as the most precious of all things and that the right to kill in self-defense must be founded on necessity?

"Do you understand that a person may repel force by force if he has reasonable ground to believe he is in danger of losing his life or suffering from great bodily harm?"

"Do you agree with the law that says a person in self-defense must not encourage the difficulty or produce the outcome.

Each juror was also asked two key questions. "Have you read or heard any information regarding the case?" and "Have you formed an opinion about the case?"

These two questions are very typical in jury selections. However, this was not a typical case. Every juror was asked whether they had heard about the case. Every one said yes. Every potential juror was asked whether they had formed an opinion. Almost every one said yes.

A "yes" answer to either question resulted in a move to strike the potential juror for cause.

Judge Faulconer, as a result of his research, granted each motion.

The seats in the jury box were numbered one through twelve. When a juror was selected, he would remain in his seat until all of the others were filled.

By the end of the day on Monday, March 16, every juror questioned had been dismissed. None had been selected. All of the seats were still awaiting occupants.

By Tuesday morning at 10:00, the newspapers, largely unfamiliar with the time consuming jury selection process, were reporting that the trial of Connie Nicholas was bogged down in jury selection. Judge Faulconer already felt the heat. He wanted desperately to do a good job in this trial and after just one day, the critics were already appearing.

The ironic thing is that he may have caused the early criticism himself. Rarely had Indianapolis had a trial even close to the scale of this one. And even then, the press was not allowed to stand in the courtroom, cameras running, microphones operating, catching every detail. So while it was not unusual for a jury trial to take a few days to complete the jury selection phase, the members of the media, relative newcomers to the judicial process, were getting antsy. They had to report something. So they reported on the tortoise-like pace of jury selection.

But by Tuesday afternoon, even Judge Faulconer was getting concerned. Still, not a single juror had been accepted by both sides. Most had been dismissed for cause. With no limit of the number of strikes available for cause, jury selection could go on for a very long time.

Wednesday came, not one juror had been seated.

The judge was letting a bit of panic creep in. How could he ever get a jury that could pass muster on the questions that were being asked? He knew that he was about to exhaust his available candidates for the jury.

By now, the press had even begun to search for other topics to write about. Instead of reciting the "blow-by-blow" account of jury selection as it had the previous two days, by Wednesday, the media was running stories about the attorney bills that Connie Nicholas was incurring and wondering how she would pay them. Connie briefly considered selling her story to a publisher. She claimed to have a few offers. Whether she truly had offers is not known. She never did sell her story.

In addition to the costs of Connie's stay in the hospital and, subsequently, her few days in jail, a new law had just been passed that increased the pay of prospective and active jurors from $5.00 per day to $7.50. In addition, the mileage allowance paid to the jurors was doubled from 5 cents to 10 cents per mile. Sheriff O'Neal estimated that his office incurred costs of $1.50 to serve a jury summons.

Already, the Connie Nicholas trial was the most expensive trial in Indiana history. And a jury was not even seated yet.

By the end of the day on Wednesday, Judge Faulconer had dismissed all 200 potential jurors originally called. At midday on Wednesday, he recognized that his supply of potential jurors was running dangerously thin. He ordered that another 175 names be drawn.

Unfortunately for Judge Faulconer, it would take a day or two to get the potential jurors called and appearing in the courtroom. He realized the bad press he might get by having to suspend the biggest trial in the country for several days after only two or three days of jury selection. He worried even more about his reputation.

The young judge had had an idea floating in his head for some time. While on the bench, contemplating his difficulties with getting a suitable jury, Judge Faulconer told the open court that he was tempted to order the sheriff's deputies to go out on the street in front of the courthouse and begin recruiting unsuspecting citizens to be jurors. In reality, it was sort of a trial balloon. But that didn't matter. He had said it.

Attorneys for both sides jumped up to object to the idea.

And from Texas to Minnesota and California to New York, the next day's headlines read, "Judge to Find Jurors On Street."

The new judge learned a new lesson. He had better watch what he said, especially in a trial like this one.

The interesting thing is that, even though he didn't do it during the Connie Nicholas trial, Judge Faulconer did that very thing in a later trial that wasn't quite as high profile. In that case, he sent his bailiff out to pick a jury from the street and upon exiting the courthouse, the bailiff saw a group standing at the corner and went directly to them.

The bailiff confidently informed the group, which turned out to be all women, that Judge Faulconer had ordered them into court for jury duty.

Little did the bailiff or judge know that the women were on a special shopping trip downtown and were standing on the corner waiting for the bus. When the bailiff grabbed them off the street, he ruined their planned day of shopping.

By the time the ladies appeared before the judge and the attorneys they were, in the judge's words, "madder than hornets." Not one of them qualified for the jury.

Judge Faulconer never picked a "street jury" again.

Thursday and Friday followed the first three unproductive days in the Connie Nicholas trial. After a full week of jury selection, the jury box was still completely empty.

Faulconer was getting more concerned. He had originally projected the trial to last two or three weeks. Now, they were a full week into the trial and were no further along.

He researched and read whatever he could find over that first weekend in an effort to find some way to break the jury selection deadlock. But he was a pioneer in this area. And pioneers don't have anyone else to compare notes with.

Nearing desperation, he consulted one of the "old-timer" attorneys in Indiana, Andrew Jacobs, Sr.

The solution that the elder attorney provided was simple. Faulconer was a bit embarrassed he hadn't thought of it.

Chapter 12

"Dear Sir: Judge Faulconer:

Would like to plead for Mrs. Connie Nicholas. Even Christ asked for forgiveness when He was on the cross for his enemies. Put the lady to work in a hospital. This would at least do some good.

Yours faithfully,
E. H. B

Letter to Judge Faulconer, 1959

All along, Faulconer had been looking for jurors who didn't know much about the case and, more importantly, hadn't formed an opinion. The fact was, no one that fit that profile existed in most of the country. Certainly not in Marion County, Indiana.

Instead, Jacobs told him, you need to find 12 jurors who, even if they have an opinion, will be able to set that opinion aside and listen objectively to the evidence.

On Monday morning, March 23, Judge Faulconer retook the bench and at 9:30 called the court to order. Jury selection would continue. Just in case it continued to take extraordinary time, he began by ordering the names of 725 more jurors drawn to be called if needed. In the pre-computer days, names were literally drawn from containers by the county clerk's staff. The trial had now consumed the names of 1100 prospective jurors in a city of less than 500,000, without a single juror being selected.

Immediately, the judge put his new strategy to work. When an attorney would ask whether a potential juror had formed an opinion and the juror would answer "yes," in response to the inevitable motion to dismiss the juror for cause, Judge Faulconer would overrule the motion until he had personally questioned the juror about his ability to set aside his opinion. A judge questioning a potential juror was far from normal. But Judge Faulconer felt this questioning was clearly within his purview in ruling on challenges to jurors for cause.

In addition, he noticed that when the room was filled with potential jurors, if one was dismissed on the basis of his answers, others who didn't want to serve would simply repeat those answers, knowing this would remove them from consideration.

The judge quickly segregated the potential jurors. He began keeping the potential jurors outside the courtroom, bringing them in one at a time for questioning. This freed many of the seats in the courtroom for spectators, although by this time, the cold weather and lack of seating and action had thinned the crowd considerably.

Within less than 48 hours, the jury had been seated. All in all, the defense had used only ten of its peremptory challenges and the prosecution had used only three.

The composition of the jury surprised everyone, elated the prosecution and caused grave concern for the defense.

Twelve married men now filled the jury box and were sworn to decide the fate of Connie Nicholas.

Even though the defense team had concern about the makeup of the jury, they tried to put the best, most confident face on. Charlie Symmes expressed confidence in the jury. Flirtatious Connie told the press that the jury was a fine looking jury and she was confident they would be fair.

Even though the court encountered slightly more difficulty in selecting the two alternates required, by the end of the week, all had been selected and sworn.

Even the alternates were married men.

Every day of jury selection and every day of the trial, the twelve jurors and two alternates dressed in white shirts, suits and ties took their numbered seats. It was obvious that these men took their civic obligation seriously.

Since the early 1970s, in virtually all criminal trials of any repute the jury is sequestered, meaning they are not allowed to go home at night. They are kept in a hotel under guard and are not allowed to watch TV or read the newspapers if any information about the case is or may be seen or heard. Sequestration of a jury is not automatic, though. Either side may request it and, absent an overriding reason, the judge will grant it, almost without exception. In a case with as much publicity as this one, sequestering the jury would certainly be the rule. But with news coverage much less pervasive in the infantile days of television, neither side requested it. The jury would go home at the end of each day of testimony and return the following day.

However, Judge Faulconer did admonish the jury at each recess, not to discuss the case or read, listen or view anything about the case.

Some jurors understandably take direction such as this more seriously than others. Early in the trial, a juror asked to see Judge Faulconer complaining that his wife was very upset with him. When the judge inquired further, the man said that, in keeping with the Judge's admonition, the juror would return home each night and lock himself in his room with a book. He felt this was the only way he could resist the temptation to discuss the case with his wife. He required his wife to bring his dinner to him in his room without discussion.

Needless to say, his wife was not pleased.

In the early stages, the press and spectators gathered in the hallways and outside the building did get to witness one admission from the star of the trial. On the second Tuesday of jury selection, during a break in the proceedings, Connie called an impromptu press conference around the defense table and admitted something very difficult for her.

For some reason, Connie was very cognizant of her age. All along she had maintained that she was 42 years old. Even her sister contended that she was 42. With press gathered with cameras pointed and bulbs flashing, Connie admitted that she had been less than truthful to this point.

She was really 44.

To many, including most of the press, this seemed like a very minor admission. However, she made this disclosure, most likely, on the advice of her attorneys. All along, Connie had maintained her age at 42, even in the face of evidence to the contrary. Routinely, one of the first questions asked of a witness is her age. If Connie Nicholas had taken the stand and given her age as 42 and the prosecution had produced her birth certificate proving her age as 44, her credibility would have been suspect from the beginning. Even if she had given her age accurately on the stand, the prosecution could have introduced her statements to the press pointing out the discrepancy. The prosecutors could have torn her apart. Any time Connie said something the prosecutors didn't like or agree with, they could bring up the lie about her age to introduce doubt about her truthfulness to the jury.

That little white lie had to be put on the table before the trial started.

Over the course of the first, then the second week of jury selection, Connie Nicholas and the press came to an understanding. She liked them and they liked her. While Judge Faulconer had placed restrictions on the press while court was in session, no such restrictions were imposed when court was in recess. So the obedient press stayed in their appointed area during the proceedings, but as soon as the judge was off the bench, they would move the cameras and recorders to the table where Connie sat and she would answer questions.

These informal press conferences infuriated Frank Symmes who warned her repeatedly to stop. She was jeopardizing the whole case, he told her. If she wanted to be defended, she better let him handle it. However, like an addiction, Connie found the attention irresistible and continued this practice throughout the entire trial, to the growing frustration of her attorneys.

With the jury selection struggle resolved, all of the parties involved returned to their homes for the long Easter weekend.

All but Connie Nicholas, that is. Connie spent her second weekend in jail.

With jury selection finally completed, both sides wondered what type of jury they had picked. The male composition seemed to favor the prosecution. But the defense had a "wild card" in the deck of jurors.

But only the juror knew it.

By Monday morning, March 30, the feel of the trial had changed and so had the weather. With a high in the middle 50s and predicted to climb each day, and the laborious jury selection finally finished, the curious began to return to the dingy basement courtroom. Opening statements were to begin in the largest trial in the country, and they wanted to witness history. The mild Monday morning also signaled what could be the beginning of the end of Connie Nicholas' life.

Although Connie was charged formally with first degree murder, which carried a maximum penalty of electrocution, the judge would also instruct the jury that they could find the defendant guilty of certain "lesser offenses" if they felt Connie's conduct did not reach the first degree murder threshold. The defense attorneys argued that the judge should tell the jury that, if the jury desired, it could convict her of as little as simple assault, a misdemeanor for which she would likely spend no time in jail. The prosecution objected strenuously. They didn't want to give the jury an easy way out. Thomason and Haggerty knew that it would be miraculous if the jury was to find that Connie Nicholas had done nothing wrong. The only real question in their minds was to what level the jury would ascribe her wrongdoing. If they could convince the judge not to allow a finding of misdemeanor assault, they were assured, they felt, of some felony conviction.

Again, the judge faced a difficult decision. He recalled that just months before, two attorneys had secured a reversal of a murder conviction for a client from the Indiana Supreme Court when it ruled that the judge should have instructed the jury that it could find the defendant guilty of lesser offenses including misdemeanor assault. This would typically mean that he was bound to follow that ruling in this case unless he could find some significant differences between that case and the one before him. What made the decision especially troublesome for Judge Faulconer was that the attorneys who had successfully argued the case before the Supreme Court were now standing before him in his courtroom. The Symmes' were fresh from that victory.

In keeping with his plan, Judge Faulconer took a short recess to ponder the appropriate action in the case. With trial notebook in hand, he pondered the ramifications of the decision. He became fairly convinced that this case was sufficiently different than the Supreme Court case such that the Appellate Court might not overrule him if he did not instruct on the lesser offenses. On the other hand, if he was wrong, he may have to try the entire case again. Plus, he would look foolish, blowing the case before it even started.

In the end, Judge Faulconer, maturing literally daily in the spotlight, put his political and selfish interests aside. He instructed the jury that they could find Mrs. Nicholas guilty of first degree murder, second degree murder, manslaughter, or, of course, they could find her not guilty. There would be no finding of guilt of a misdemeanor.

He had now made two decisions that he hoped would not give an appellate court grounds to reverse him.

By now, the trial was the talk of Indianapolis and the world. Newspapers large and small from all over the United States clamored for angles on the Connie Nicholas trial. But the fascination now extended beyond the borders of the U.S. Reporters from papers from Australia to Japan and Germany were arriving, poised to cover the proceedings. Water coolers and coffee machines were abuzz with opinions of Connie's guilt or innocence and predictions of the jury's verdict.

As the tedious jury selection process reached it conclusion, an envelope arrived at the Marion County Prosecutor's Office addressed to Mr. Philip Bayt, Prosecutor. The return address was from California. In it was a letter from a witness to whom Bayt had issued a subpoena to testify for the state at the trial.

Sounding more like an RSVP for a party, Laura Mowrer was writing to say, quite simply, that she "unfortunately will not be able to attend" the trial.

When Laura had fled Indianapolis months before, her lawyer, David Lewis had declined to say where she had gone. She had family on the East Coast, and that was where most observers assumed she had gone. In reality, her relatives were in Connecticut, and, in the execution of Mr. Lewis' plan, that wouldn't be far enough away.

David Lewis knew the law. When he created the master plan to have Laura make a statement then leave town, he knew exactly what he was doing. Indiana law included a provision in the 1950's that allowed the state to require the presence of a witness in a criminal trial who was located within 1000 miles of the state. As travel was much more difficult and much less frequent in the first half of the century, application of this law was rarely an issue. However, it would have a definite impact on the Connie Nicholas trial.

Connecticut was less than 1000 miles away. California wasn't.

Phil Bayt could not legally require Laura Mowrer to return from California. Laura Mowrer would not be part of the trial of Connie Nicholas.

Both sides expressed their disappointment. The prosecution had hoped to use Laura's testimony to help prove Connie's preoccupation and premeditation by showing that she routinely called Mowrer's apartment, hanging up as soon as the phone was answered. The defense had hoped that Miss Mowrer's testimony would cause sympathy for Connie in the eyes of the jury.

Neither side would get the chance.

In reality, Laura had done things her way after all. She wanted to let the police know what had happened and, through her secret meeting before leaving town, she had accomplished that. She had then fled to California before her face was on the front page of the Indianapolis newspapers. And by the time the case became front page news in California, her name had faded from the headlines.

On Tuesday morning, after a Monday session comprised largely of pre-trial jury instructions and meetings with the attorneys in the judge's cramped, dark chambers, the public finally saw what they came for. Deputy Prosecutor Francis Thomason's opening statement took the jurors on a lively, brash retrospective of the relationship of Connie Nicholas and Forrest Teel.

"Teel was always gentle with the defendant. She accepted monetary and other gifts from him. She accepted all he could offer her under the circumstances," Thomason said, forcefully.

Then he said, quietly, "In return she fired three death-laden bullets into his body and gave him a bed on a cold, hard slab in the city morgue."

The courtroom was silent as he continued.

"Regardless of what might have been written or said, the moral aspect of her relationship with Forrest Teel is not the issue in this case," Thomason continued. But he couldn't resist pointing out the moral depravity, just in case anyone was interested.

They were.

"The evidence will show that a number of years ago, she and Forrest Teel became acquainted when they worked at the same place of business, that both were married persons and that they became on intimate terms!" he recounted, his voice rising.

The courtroom was enthralled by the near-evangelical oration.

The out-of-control white Cadillac of Forrest Teel was finally stopped when it hit a utility pole. This picture was taken as medical personnel were arriving, only to find that the car's occupant had died while they were en route.

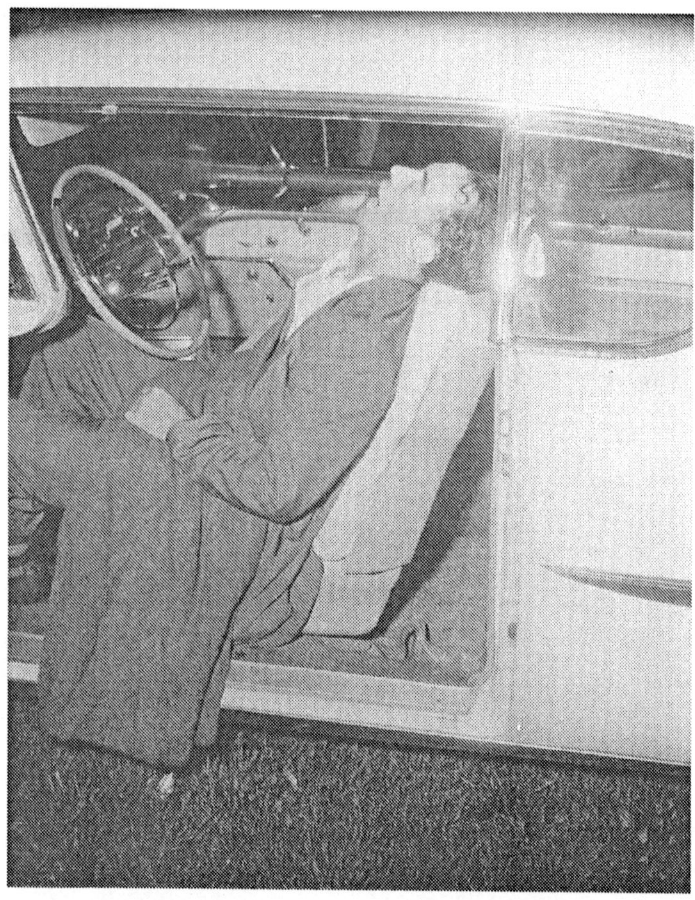

Forrest Teel lay in his flashy white Cadillac, mortally wounded by an unknown assailant. The blanket in his lap was placed there by police as they awaited the arrival of the ambulance. Alive when found, Teel steadfastly refused to betray the identity of his killer.

This is the evidence photo used in the trial showing the inside of Forrest Teel's white Cadillac after the shooting. The prosecution has circled the indentation on the driver's door caused by the one shot that missed Teel, struck the door and fell to the floor.

Connie was found the evening after Forrest Teel was killed near Fall Creek. She was unconscious and doctors later discovered she had ingested at least 75 sleeping pills mixed into a paste with some pineapple juice. This photo was taken shortly after police arrived on the scene and shows the position she was in when she was found. She later claimed that hours of pressure from her head resting on her arms caused the injury to her left hand. During the trial, she claimed that a scuffle over the gun had caused the injury to the right hand.

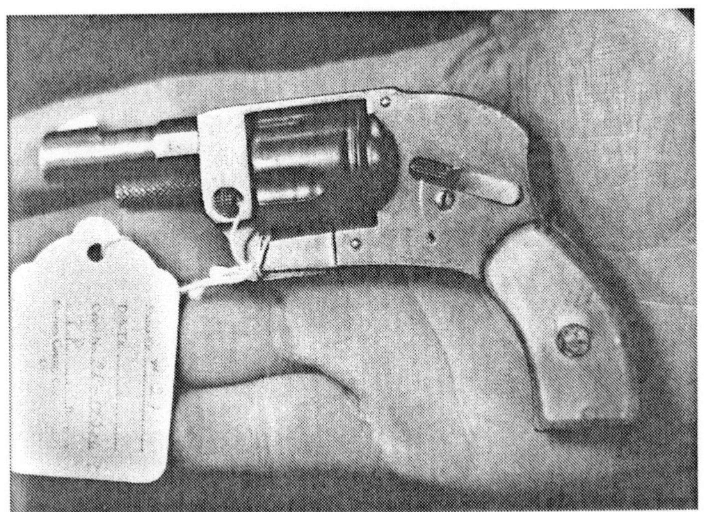

The choice of this rare, French-made revolver would ultimately make the case easier to tie to Connie Nicholas. The pawn shop owner strongly recommended a more common .22 caliber pistol, but Connie insisted on this small five-shot model. The trigger is folded up into the gun in this photo. Life Magazine photo by Michael Rougier/TimePix.

With a few exceptions, prior to the beginning of testimony each day, hopeful spectators lined the dark, dingy basement hallway trying to secure one of the few coveted seats in the courtroom for the day. Life Magazine photo by Michael Rougier/TimePix.

The packed courtroom was lighted by bare fluorescent lights that hung from the ceiling. The exposed pipes on the wall led to radiators that would make various sounds during the trial. This photo clearly shows some of the pedestrians who were constant fixtures at the windows during the trial.

Cameras and reporters vied for position in the small space allocated to the press during the trial. As the trial climaxed, the space became more and more crowded.

Judge Faulconer, only 35 years old and trying the biggest case of his career, addresses one of the attorneys on the case. The Connie Nicholas trial was the first murder case the judge had been involved in any capacity and, in actuality, was the first he had ever seen.

Life Magazine photo by Michael Rougier/TimePix.

Attorneys listen to Judge Faulconer during a sidebar conference. Closest to the bench are Jud Haggerty (with hand to face), Joe Quill and Charlie Symmes. Behind Jud is Phil Bayt. Francis Thomason is next to Bayt and Frank Symmes has his back to the camera.

Life Magazine photo by Michael Rougier/TimePix.

Connie glances around the courtroom during one of the frequent recesses. One of the elaborate braces fitted to her hands is clearly visible in this photo. Many spectators as well as members of the prosecution felt that the emotional outbursts and the hand braces were both carefully designed to evoke sympathy from the all-male jury. Life Magazine photo by Michael Rougier/TimePix.

Handsome, young Jud Haggerty confers with Phil Bayt, Joe Quill and Frank Symmes in front of the judge's bench. Life Magazine photo by Michael Rougier/TimePix.

During the frequent recesses, the rules for the press were suspended. Here, defense attorney Frank Symmes addresses the defendant, Connie Nicholas while cameramen and reporters maneuver to get the best angle. Very often, Connie would invite the press to come to the defense table during breaks and she would hold impromptu press conferences, much to the dismay and objection of her defense team. Life Magazine photo by Michael Rougier/TimePix.

Like the courtroom itself, the judge's chambers were fit wherever there was room when the court was built. This caused for cramped quarters when the attorneys were called into chambers for discussions and hearings outside of the courtroom. Clockwise from left: Charlie Symmes, Phil Bayt, Frank Symmes, Francis Thomason, Joe Quill, Jud Haggerty and Judge Faulconer. Court bailiff Fred Titus is barely visible behind Thomason. Life Magazine photo by Michael Rougier/TimePix.

Charlie Symmes stresses his main points to the jury during final arguments. Later in the trial, the defense and prosecution tables were moved to face the jury rather than the judge. Life Magazine photo by Michael Rougier/TimePix.

At the end of the trial, as the jury deliberated in an adjacent room, attorneys, court personnel and spectators looked for ways to pass the time. Near the bottom of the picture, two people have chosen the jurors' chairs to wait, propping their feet on the railing. Just out of view, another person has done the same in the judge's chair on the bench. Notice the wiring on the wall near the top-center of the picture. As more and more motion picture photographers attended the trial, the current electrical cabling in the courtroom became woefully inadequate. Life Magazine photo by Michael Rougier/TimePix.

Thomason's opening statement lasted only 10 minutes, but was very effective. The room was completely still and quiet with the exception of the constant sobs of the defendant.

"Connie Nicholas committed a vicious, well-schemed, calculated murder," he said before taking his seat at the prosecution table furthest from the judge, but closest to the jury and spectators.

The slight Charlie Symmes handled the opening statement for the defense. In a much more conversational tone, Symmes simply and frankly explained the defendant's actions as the defense would portray them to the men of the jury.

She was a jilted mistress bent on killing herself when her lover suddenly, unpredictably became violent, he said.

"She got the gun out and said she was going to kill herself," he said. "He said, 'Don't be a damned fool' and grabbed her arm. In the struggle the gun went off four times."

He went on to outline Connie's troubled childhood, implicitly illustrating her lifelong search for lifelong security.

Each side's opening statement was surprisingly brief. They each got to the point, and sat down.

Like a championship boxer, the prosecution team started the presentation of its case with some light jabs, toying with the defense, softening the opponent for what was to come later.

The first witness called to the stand was Mrs. Edna Smith.

Mrs. Smith, a sixth grade teacher who lived across the hall from Laura Mowrer, looked every bit the part of her vocation. She was a thin woman, on the far side of middle age, wearing somewhat outdated light blue cat's eye glasses and pearls. She sported a square, brimmed hat reminiscent of a political convention. The hat remained perched on her head during the entirety of her testimony.

Mrs. Smith was an important witness, and although many in the crowd didn't realize it, she was able to offer some testimony very damaging to Connie Nicholas. She was able to testify about hearing the loud, excited voices of the two arguing lovers and, more importantly, talked at some length about the gunshots that she heard that previous July night. Deputy Prosecutor Thomason questioned Mrs. Smith again and again about the noises she had heard. At first, she thought they were teenagers with some post-Fourth of July firecrackers.

One of the most important things that Mrs. Smith said was that there were several seconds between "explosions," as she called them. She testified clearly and distinctly that she heard two shots with a brief intermission between of about a second. She then heard two more shots, spaced further apart, perhaps three of four seconds apart.

Few in the courtroom appreciated the importance of Thomason's line of questioning. But the implication was clear to the attorneys and, the prosecution hoped, to the jurors. If Connie had really fired the gun in self-defense, the shots would have been closer together. Alternatively, if the shooting had been accidental, the spacing made even less sense. The space between shots indicated that Connie shot Teel deliberately.

According to the prosecution, Mrs. Smith's testimony was irrefutable proof of the premeditation of Connie's crime.

Mrs. Smith also told the jury that she saw someone leave the white Cadillac after the shooting, but she was unable to identify the person. In fact, she was unsure if the person fleeing was male or female.

A jury trial requires a much different touch for an attorney than does a bench trial. A bench trial requires only that the attorneys elicit the key facts from witnesses. The judge, trained in the law just as the attorneys are, will be able to ignore extraneous evidence, such as opinions, from witness testimony.

In a jury trial, however, the attorneys have very little idea what the jury will disregard, if anything. Therefore, they must object to inadmissible evidence promptly, if possible, before the jury even hears it.

But there is another side to that strategy. If objections are made too frequently by one side, the jury will begin to believe that the objecting party has something to hide. In reality, this may well not be true. But truth is often not the central issue in a jury trial. What matters is what the jury *believes* to be true.

A good lawyer knows that there is a big difference between those two possibilities.

So while the defense could have brutally grilled Mrs. Smith, in reality, she only said one thing that was of any consequence during her testimony, how far apart the shots were spaced. Her testimony of her actions prior to the shooting made absolutely no difference to the guilt or innocence of Connie Nicholas. Even her testimony about seeing someone leave the Cadillac did no damage, since she could not even determine the gender of the person. Therefore, the defense team simply left this portion of her testimony alone.

Charlie Symmes made an admirable attempt to shake Mrs. Smith's recollection of the timing of the shots. But, despite cross-examination, Charlie Symmes was unable to introduce any doubt or inconsistency to the witness' story.

Mrs. Smith was allowed off the stand.

The second witness for the prosecution was Patrolman Anderson, the first policeman on the scene of the accident. The policeman, in a monotone reminiscent of Sgt. Joe Friday of Dragnet, the popular television show in 1959, yet riveting nonetheless, told of receiving the radio call at 1:06 AM to the scene of a personal injury accident and, instead, finding a man slumped in his luxury car, mortally wounded with three gunshot wounds.

"There was sweat on his forehead, sweat on his hands. His skin was clammy," he testified. He reached forward, grabbing Teel by the shoulder and pulling him back in the seat.

Anderson repeatedly asked for the victim's name, but he refused to give it. The officer asked multiple times who the shooter was, but Teel refused to divulge that information as well.

He also testified that despite Teel's condition, he would have been able to respond.

The prosecution had, in a roundabout way, just told the jury that, most likely, Teel knew his assailant. This fact was, of course, already known, as Connie had not denied shooting the man. However, it was still quite dramatic.

Plus, the revelations did serve one crucial purpose.

The prosecution was attempting to prove that Forrest Teel was a kind, caring companion to Connie Nicholas. In fact, he was so compassionate toward her, that he would rather die than name her as his killer. A gentlemen, at least in some regards.

Was that the type of man that would hit her?

Charlie Symmes conducted an abbreviated cross-examination of the patrolman, eliciting little new information. Again, the facts introduced by the lawman's testimony produced little damage to the defense's case. Everyone knew that Teel had been at the wheel of the car as it careened out of control and crashed. No one was disputing that he died at the scene. Indeed, Connie had already admitted to police and the rest of the world that she had shot him.

Charlie Symmes went appropriately easy on the Patrolman.

Patrolman Anderson was followed on the stand by his supervisor, Lt. London. Lt. London reiterated the course of events that the patrolman had previously outlined. The lieutenant did, however, recount the moments just before the victim's death.

"I saw him struggling for life. He lived four or five minutes and died," the veteran lawman said quietly and matter-of-factly.

Earl Alexander, the neighbor who was among the first to arrive at the scene was next and recounted what he had witnessed that early morning after being awakened by the screeching tires. He recounted in detail his hurriedly getting dressed, his race to the scene and his arrival at the disabled Cadillac.

The defense offered no cross-examination for either Lt. London or Earl Alexander. Again, none was needed.

By now, the novice judge was feeling better. He had a jury, the trial was under way, and, with one minor exception, the press was strictly following the rules he had laid out prior to the trial. Shortly after the trial began, one of the cameramen from a national news organization turned on his motion picture camera. It was noticeably louder than the others. Judge Faulconer immediately ordered the camera shut off. He instructed the gentleman in the press area to his right that if he could find a quieter camera, he would be welcome back. But that particular camera was outside the limitations the judge had set earlier.

At the next recess, several members of the judge's staff told him, in no uncertain terms, that ejecting the cameraman was a huge mistake. After all, national news organizations could provide publicity for the judge that could extend, literally around the world! He should have treated the cameraman better, they said.

Judge Faulconer simply told them he had no choice, and, frankly, he didn't care who the camera belonged to. It was unclear whether he really believed that. The staff braced for a backlash.

Luckily, none came. In the end, shortly after the recess, the camera operator returned with a newer, quieter camera. Nothing more was said about the incident by the cameraman, the judge or his staff.

That incident simply exaggerated the good feeling the judge had about the trial at that point.

Unfortunately, like much of Judge Faulconer's career to this point, the good feeling wouldn't last long.

An omen of things to come came in a phone call to the Judge days later. During his pre-trial preparation and during the first phase of the trial, Judge Faulconer had become good friends with the WFBM-TV anchorman, Ken Myers. They would talk at times about the trial and the press coverage and, during those first few days, together, they agreed on small adjustments to the judge's rules. However, overall, Judge Faulconer was quite pleased with the behavior of the press and the lack of effect media coverage was having on the trial itself.

Part of that satisfaction was the knowledge that the judge had that an experienced news professional was never more than a phone call, or even just a few blocks away.

But when Judge Faulconer answered the phone late that afternoon after court had recessed for the day, he would be told that Ken Myers had died unexpectedly.

In the middle of the biggest case of his life, Judge Faulconer had lost a friend, mentor and advisor. Too late to change his mind about press coverage, the judge would have to go it alone from here on.

The next witness that the prosecution called to the stand was the doctor who had performed the autopsy on the victim. Dr. Emmett Pierce, age 36, a small, stocky man with a short haircut, round face and light horn-rimmed glasses looked very professional as he strode to the witness stand in a tweed suit on that Wednesday morning. The heat of the courtroom and the enormity of the case would conspire to make the doctor regret his wardrobe choice.

Dr. Pierce was a resident in pathology at General Hospital, having graduated from medical school in 1952. Although his primary function at the hospital was examining and interpreting tissue slides, he was also a participant in a rotation of doctors who did autopsies at the hospital. The night that Forrest Teel's body was brought to the hospital, Dr. Pierce was the doctor assigned to do autopsies at that time.

General Hospital had been a fixture in Indianapolis for many years. Other than a simple name change from City Hospital a few years earlier, the hospital remained much the same. Physically, the original building was still in use, although certain departments had been moved within it over the history of the facility.

The morgue and autopsy room were located on the fourth floor, a bit strange as most were relegated to the hospital basement at the time. It was clear that this space was not originally designed for this purpose. The room in which autopsies were conducted was more like an amphitheater. It was windowless and contained approximately 5 rows of risers, such as would be found in a high school gymnasium, in an "L"-shape looking down on the autopsy table. Autopsies were not often spectator events, and over the years, doctors had begun to use the benches as shelves to hold various human organs in jars filled with formaldehyde. By 1958, the risers were completely filled with hundreds of the bottles and the odor was quite strong.

Dr. Pierce was joined by orderlies, who dutifully undressed the body in preparation for the procedure, and representatives of the police, who watched the autopsy as part of the investigation. Dr. Pierce wondered why Teel's pants were unzipped, but no one in the room knew the answer.

By the time the doctor first examined the body, he had already been informed that the deceased was a very important person at Eli Lilly, although his name meant nothing to the doctor at the time.

That would change over the next several months.

Although autopsies were part of Dr. Pierce's job as a pathology resident, he, like the others, did not necessarily look forward to the critical and all-too-frequent task. General Hospital was one of three hospitals in the city conducting autopsies and Dr. Pierce and his colleagues averaged about two or three a day. Since each one took about two hours, often, little else could be accomplished by the doctor on duty.

In order to make the job more tolerable, the hospital began paying the doctors a "bonus" of $25 per autopsy. They received more if the case went to trial and the doctor was forced to testify.

Dr. Emmett Pierce and his young family were $50 richer that day, thanks to the murder of Forrest Teel.

The doctor, in cold, technical terms, told the court that Mr. Teel was shot three times. Although the doctor could not definitively pinpoint the order in which the bullets entered the body, he was able to specifically identify three bullet wounds. The first bullet had entered the body between the fifth and sixth rib on the right side, crossed through the intestines and lodged just below the eighth rib on the left side. The second bullet also entered the victim on the right side just above the hipbone, and lodged on the left side near the sixth rib. The third bullet entered the man's neck, also on the right side, ricocheted off some bone, and came to rest in his left shoulder.

The second bullet he identified was the one that killed him. According to the doctor, the bullet that entered near the hip had lacerated his liver. That was the official cause of death and was duly noted on the death certificate.

Connie sobbed, sometimes uncontrollably during Pierce's testimony.

When Thomason handed the doctor the bullets extracted from the body and asked him to identify them, the defendant broke down.

The prosecution had one more question for Dr. Pierce.

Thomason asked the doctor for his opinion on the angle of the bullets. If the angle of the bullets showed that Teel was facing the windshield at the time of the shooting, it would have been impossible for him to be hitting Connie and grabbing her arm at the time he was shot.

Before the question was even completed by Thomason, all three defense attorneys were on their feet strenuously objecting. They had been anticipating this question. Pierce was a doctor, they said, and should only be allowed to testify about medical information, not speculate about the position of the body when he was shot.

The judge had to consider both sides of the argument.

Clearly, based on his medical knowledge, the doctor would know which way the bullets entered the body. The path the bullets took through the body would, without question, indicate the direction Mr. Teel was facing at the time he was shot.

On the other hand, the doctor was not at the scene, had not witnessed the shooting and was offering the answer based on purely circumstantial evidence, not something he witnessed.

A jury trial should be in the hands of the jury. A decision by the judge should not sway the outcome in favor of one side or another, he thought. Like an umpire or other official in a sporting event, the judge should try not to affect the outcome.

The judge thought for a moment. The attorneys awaited the decision. Judge Faulconer looked at the clock. Luckily, it was getting later in the day. He bought himself some time to sort things out.

Judge Faulconer recessed court until Thursday morning at which time he would make his ruling.

As soon as the judge left the courtroom, the assembled media swarmed the doctor, asking him what his answer would be. He refused to say.

That evening, Judge Faulconer struggled with whether to allow the testimony of the doctor. What the doctor had to say was definitely important and would be helpful to the jury in deciphering the events of that evening.

However, if he admitted the testimony over the objection of the defense, that could potentially be grounds for the defense to mount a successful appeal. That could, again, affect the fragile reputation of the young judge, not to mention cause him to try the case all over again, from jury selection forward.

He had to make the right decision. Unfortunately, he wouldn't know if it was the right decision until the case was over and, if the case was appealed, an appellate court had ruled. He poured over his trial notebook. It offered little guidance.

The next morning, Judge Faulconer took the bench, took a deep breath and announced that Dr. Emmett Pierce was not qualified to answer the question and, therefore, would not be allowed to answer it.

He also instructed the jury to disregard the question.

Even though it appeared the defense team had won that battle, in fact, the prosecution team may have won the war. The doctor was able to testify, medically, that all the shots had entered the body from the right side traversing across the body to the left, rather than front to back, a more likely path in a self defense shooting. Plus, even though the jury was told to ignore the question, they had heard it and the prosecution team knew that completely ignoring it would be impossible for the jury.

Relief washed over the judge as he leaned back in his chair.

It would be short-lived once again.

By now, the novice jury had come to expect the frequent delays, although they didn't quite understand the reason sometimes. For the most part, the judge was checking on himself before making an important ruling, but the jury, no member having served on a jury before, assumed this was normal behavior and did not question it, even among themselves.

They simply dutifully paraded through a short hallway to the jury room and waited, under the watchful eye of one of the two court bailiffs until the judge instructed them to return.

On the morning of the second day, the jury was instructed to leave the courtroom for a legal argument. As the last juror, number 12, filed into the rectangular room and took seats around the conference table in the center, one of the jurors, to the relief of the others, produced a deck of cards from his pocket.

Bridge, being the game of choice, they would get plenty of practice during the next few weeks.

The prosecution next called Lt. Joseph Hunt. Lt. Hunt was an employee of the Indianapolis Police Department and was a regionally well-known ballistics expert. He had the serious look and build of a bulldog and a thick head of black, curly hair. During the course of Lt. Hunt's testimony, the courtroom was shown a strange looking chart that had the look of an astronomy chart more than anything associated with a murder weapon. Light gray streaks traveled from left to right on the rectangular display. It was longer than it was tall. The background was blotchy and a slightly darker gray. The chart was actually an enlarged close-up picture of a bullet fired by the tiny French revolver. Lt. Hunt compared the picture to another picture, this one of the bullets fired into the body of Forrest Teel.

The pictures were identical. The lieutenant was able to link the fatal bullets to the small revolver found with Connie the night she attempted suicide.

In truth, the ballistics evidence was not earth-shattering. Everyone already knew that the bullets would match. But it made for some good press and also made an impression on the jury.

The lieutenant's testimony would not, however, be entirely without controversy.

Deputy Prosecutor Jud Haggerty next questioned the lieutenant about the gun itself. Holding the murder weapon in his hand, the lieutenant described the gun and it was entered into evidence. But when Haggerty asked the witness to describe "how the trigger pulls," once again, all three defense attorneys were out of their seats objecting before the question was even finished.

Wily Frank Symmes took the lead in voicing the objection to the question. Symmes lobbied Judge Faulconer, claiming that allowing the witness to answer would "invade the province of the jury."

The judge debated the point in his head for a brief time. He quickly realized the response to the objection was not going to be formulated easily. He ordered the jury removed from the room once again.

After removing the jury from the room, the judge heard arguments for both sides.

Following strenuous argument from both sides, and a brief consultation with his brown trial notebook, Judge Faulconer eventually agreed with the defense. The lieutenant could not answer that question.

During the short recess while the jury was in another room, the judge allowed the press to examine the gun. Members of the press eagerly handled the deceptively small gun with fascination. But as they began to pull the trigger, they were all shocked.

Most guns require little pressure to squeeze the trigger. Although different guns require different amounts of pressure to fire, most handguns will fire with about two pounds of pressure on the trigger. Some require less and earn the distinction of a "hair" trigger. Others require more. However, it is quite extraordinary for a gun to require more than four and a half to five pounds of pressure.

Connie's gun took seven pounds of pressure to fire.

The equally crafty, if not quite as experienced, Jud Haggerty, having lost his bid to have Lt. Hunt give his opinion to the jury as to the difficulty in firing the gun, had another card up his sleeve. If the judge accepted Haggerty's next suggestion, the exclusion of Lt. Hunt's testimony might be of no consequence.

Haggerty asked the judge for permission to allow the jury to handle the gun with the instruction that they should pull the trigger.

Again, the defense attorneys leapt from their seats, almost yelling their objection.

"A jury has no right to experiment with the evidence," a visibly frustrated Frank Symmes maintained. "A jury must accept the evidence as it comes from the witness stand,"

Again, the judge was at a crossroads. The evidence the prosecution was seeking to introduce was very important. The fact that it took so much pressure to fire the gun was a clear indication that an accidental shooting was unlikely.

The accidental discharge four times seemed a near impossibility.

However, for the judge, the bigger issue was the legal one. Legally, could he instruct the jury to pull the trigger on the gun? Should he instruct them to do so?

The testimony of Lt. Hunt and the legal wrangling that followed had consumed the better part of the day. The jury remained locked in their back room, no doubt wondering what was going on in the courtroom that they were not allowed to hear as they played hand after hand of Bridge. Once again, the judge took the opportunity to consider the motion overnight. He ordered his bailiff to send the grateful jurors home for the evening.

Friday morning, the final day of the first week of testimony was looming. Judge Faulconer was no closer to a decision on the jury's handling of the gun. He had spent the evening researching the issue and had found no guidance. He considered both sides over and over again with no resolution. He was torn between the interests of a fair trial for the defendant, the truth for the jury and possibly having to relive the toughest trial of his life over in a few months.

Early Friday morning, Judge Faulconer had an epiphany.

At 9:30 on Friday morning, Judge Faulconer called the courtroom to order. The press, the attorneys, the spectators and even the defendant, all now knowing the importance of the trigger on the gun waited restlessly. The members of the press, having handled the gun and pulled the stiff trigger the day before, had led their daily coverage in the morning papers with stories about the hard pull of the trigger. Everyone in the courtroom knew the gravity of the decision that was being made by the Judge. Everyone but the jury, who, upon reporting for duty that morning, were immediately taken to the deliberation room once again.

To the hushed courtroom, the judge then announced that he would allow the jury to handle the gun. However, he would make no order, recommendation or suggestion to them as to whether the trigger may be pulled.

Neither side was sure what that ruling meant. For that matter, neither was the judge. No one, including Judge Faulconer was sure who had won that round.

They didn't have to wait long for the victor to be crowned.

Judge Faulconer ordered the jury returned to the jury box. He then allowed Haggerty to present the gun to the jury for examination.

Haggerty handed the gun to the bailiff, who, in turn, presented it to the juror seated in chair #1. The juror took the gun and immediately gripped it in his right hand, grimacing with exertion. The courtroom was still and quiet, interrupted only by two clicks of the gun as the man pulled the trigger twice. As he passed the weapon to his left, the next juror also pulled the trigger.

In all, the trigger of the gun was pulled thirty-four times. Many grimaced as they attempted to squeeze the reluctant trigger. Some used both hands.

Seven pounds of pressure is significant. The force required to fire the weapon is comparable to the force required to pick up a full gallon of milk. Doing so with one finger was no simple task, even for the grown men of the jury.

Frank Symmes was furious. At the end of the examination of the gun by the jury, he immediately leapt to his feet, demanding that the judge declare a mistrial. "The jury has no right to experiment with the evidence," he reiterated.

Judge Faulconer quickly and confidently overruled the motion for a mistrial.

The fact is, this was, at last, an easy decision for the judge. Juries experiment with evidence all the time. The only difference this time was that they were doing it in the courtroom. Typically, they do it in the jury room.

The prosecution celebrated its victory.

The prosecution also introduced another interesting piece of evidence. On the night of Connie's unsuccessful suicide attempt, police searched the blue and white 1955 Chevrolet and inventoried the items contained inside it. One item, plainly in view on the dashboard of the car, was a 3" by 5" index card, creased in the center as if it had been kept in a pocket. The card contained two typewritten lines:

> 2922 E. 29th Street, Apt. 638
> Laura L. Mowrer—Li. 7-8824

Connie had added her phone number at the bottom of the card.

In the meantime, at each recess, Connie continued her press conferences. She clearly was enjoying the spotlight in spite of the reason it was shining on her. And even though her defense attorneys did not particularly approve of her actions, it wasn't long before they realized that her conversations were actually helping her cause.

One of the crucial strategies a defense attorney must employ is the humanization of his client. A jury is much more likely to convict a defendant that they see only as the defendant than it is to convict a "person" who may have committed a crime. Consequently, competent defense attorneys refer to their clients by their first name, or nickname. They often place their hand on shoulder of the defendant while talking about him. They try to bring in personal information wherever possible.

Ironically, as the press ran stories about Connie around the world, public opinion began to shift behind the jilted lover.

As the trial progressed, fewer people were predicting harsh penalties for the defendant. Indeed, many were now beginning to predict an outright acquittal.

One member of the defense team still was not sold on the idea of Connie talking to the press, however. Frank Symmes was from the old school. Defendants shouldn't talk, he thought. And he reminded Connie frequently.

"I told you to keep your mouth shut," Frank Symmes snapped on more than one occasion during the trial. Later in the case, he began adding the comment, "I keep telling you that, but I guess you don't want to pay any attention to me."

Connie usually just shrugged her shoulders and went on about her business, inviting the press back to the table at the very next break.

By now, the word had begun to spread that the jury selection was over and the spectators began to return to the trial. And so did the press. Several newspapers compared the scene to the end of the month sale at a department store. Representatives from media in Louisville, Chicago, and New York had now set up permanent residence in the courthouse and were observing and reporting on every day of the trial. Some organizations even laid unauthorized claims to hallway coat closets and other storage spaces and had their own dedicated telephone lines run right into the courthouse.

Even Judge Faulconer gave up his small, cramped office at certain times to allow members of the press to phone their stories in before deadlines. When asked about the presence of so many reporters, the judge was quoted as saying, "If we have to handle anymore reporters, I don't know where we will put them."

It would get worse.

Chapter 13

"Women Eat, Watch and Weep."
Indianapolis Star
April 8, 1959

The composition of the jury was in stark contrast to the make-up of the spectators that began, once again, to line the dingy tiled hallway hoping to secure one of the coveted seats during the twice-a-day seating. Of the fifty available seats, typically no more than two would be occupied by men. Part of the reason is explained by the time. In 1959, most all men worked during the day and a significant portion of the female population did not. Therefore, females had more time to spend an entire day watching the proceedings. However, in addition to the sociological explanation, the plain fact is that women were more fascinated with the murderous defendant. They strained to catch glimpses of her through the doors and windows. She galvanized the feelings of women across the country. She was either admired or hated. Other women were simply not ambivalent about Connie Nicholas.

By the women in the courtroom, Connie was clearly more hated than admired. As Connie sobbed, the women in attendance did not join her. Instead, they gave disapproving looks as though she was simply acting, trying to invoke the sympathy of the jury. When she laughed, few would laugh with her.

Even the wire services began reporting on the cold reception that Connie received from the predominately female courtroom.

To this day, many older women in Indianapolis are quick to voice deep-seated negative opinions of the little adulteress. Ironically, these same women often express sympathy for Laura Mowrer. "Connie ruined the man's marriage. She couldn't be trusted. She should have known better than to play around with a married man," they would say. But poor little Laura was in the wrong place at the wrong time. She was taken advantage of by that older man." The fact that each of them was involved in the same way with the same man was lost.

As the weather naturally warmed during the course of the trial through the inevitable approach of spring, the old un-airconditioned courthouse became musty, close and uncomfortable. The pedestal fans located in opposite corners provided little comfort on especially warm days, merely moving around the hot, sticky air.

Many days, the judge ordered the windows opened. However, even this proved to be more than he bargained for. On at least one occasion, a group of what were believed to be young girls pushed their way to the front of the crowd at one of the windows and yelled greetings to Connie through the open glass.

The judge ordered the bailiff to investigate, but the perpetrators were gone before the bailiff could make the trip out of the courtroom and up the stairs.

In spite of the interruptions, the windows remained open most of the time. There was little choice, really.

In addition to the breeze sporadically provided by the open windows, members of the court staff and sometimes even other spectators would routinely take turns delivering water to the gallery, welcome refreshment to the fashionable women overdressed for the weather in hats, gloves and long dresses.

Rarely does a defendant in a criminal case testify on his or her own behalf. To put it more accurately, rarely will a defense attorney allow a defendant to testify.

In spite of the Constitutional right of the Fifth Amendment against self-incrimination, most laypersons assume that when a defendant declines to testify, that person is hiding something. In some cases, jurors may even assume guilt just because the defendant did not testify. But the truth is, when a defendant takes the stand, she opens herself up to questions that she would not have to deal with if she stays seated at the defense table and keeps her mouth shut.

Simply put, when a defendant takes the stand, the prosecution has the Constitutional right to cross-examine her. And that cross-examination can, and most likely, will, include questions about the defendant's past, character and conduct, not to mention the details of the crime that the defense would prefer not to discuss.

Political campaigns are sufficient proof that almost everyone has some unfortunate and less than tasteful incidents in the past. A good attorney can make them look even worse.

In Connie's case, she had plenty of baggage by this point in her life. Taking the stand meant she could be asked virtually any question about the shooting, but also questions about her two divorces, a somewhat scandalous position in its own right in the 50s, any other affairs she had, and even specific questions about her 15-year relationship with the man she had killed. And once she opened herself up by taking the stand, her Fifth Amendment right to quit answering questions would be limited.

Putting Connie Nicholas on the stand was the last thing the defense team wanted to do. Still, the more they thought about the advantages and disadvantages, the more they felt as though they had to put her on the stand. They were betting that the charismatic defendant could convince the men in the jury box that she was telling the truth, despite empirical evidence to the contrary. After all, she had been able to convince a hardened veteran policeman of her innocence while in the hospital. Hopefully the same tactics would work on the twelve men in the jury box.

Yet the decision was still far from clear. The defense was in a true dilemma. If they didn't allow Connie to testify, they would have a very tough time overcoming the already damaging evidence of the path of the bullets and the incredible pressure it took to fire the gun.

On the other hand, Connie may be eaten alive by the venerable prosecution team.

The defense attorneys constantly debated the merit of putting Connie on the stand. Their decision changed frequently as the case progressed.

Ultimately, they decided they had to take the chance.

As the rumors began to spread by the end of the week that Connie may, indeed, take the stand in her own defense, interest in the trial skyrocketed. Attending the trial in the tiny courtroom became a social event. The number of reporters almost doubled.

Somehow, the judge did find a way to accommodate the additional reporters. But they weren't exactly comfortable. The ever-increasing number was packed tighter and tighter into the space originally allotted to the press to the right of the judge in the courtroom. Eventually, Judge Faulconer had little choice but to give a few of the front row seats to them as well. Throughout, he made sure the local press was favored.

Connie wasn't ready for the stand yet, though. The prosecution wasn't quite done. They had a couple more bombshells to lob before they went on the defensive.

The young-looking, crew-cut Ralph Gano was on the stand near the end of the day on Friday. Standing out in an open collar shirt, sharp contrast to the proper dress of everyone else in the courtroom, witness and spectator alike, in a very relaxed way, he related the phone call and visits from Connie Nicholas the previous July. He talked about her decision to purchase the small, French revolver over the more standard .22 caliber Gano had recommended. He made sure the jury knew that she had repeatedly told the shopkeeper of her plans to go to California.

The prosecution team was also able to use Mr. Gano to reinforce several issues involving the gun. Gano agreed with Lt. Hunt's unheard assertion that it was a difficult gun to fire. He also repeatedly asserted that the gun required distinct, separate pulls of the trigger to fire repeatedly.

The fact that the trigger had to be pulled each time the gun fired was of importance as well. Since the gun was fired four times, Gano's testimony meant that Connie had to have made the decision to fire each time. Once again, she had the opportunity to stop, and didn't.

Connie's version of the shooting looked to be in trouble.

And the prosecution still wasn't done.

The next two witnesses were Det. Michaelis and Det. Smith, both of whom interviewed the defendant within a short time of her stirring from her coma. The appearance of the two policemen caused another tactical dilemma for the defense team. Frank and Charlie Symmes knew that the policemen would testify about their interrogation of the defendant and, specifically, bring out the details of her confession. A basic strategy for most defenses is to attempt to convince the judge to exclude any confession by the defendant. This can often be done on one of several grounds.

However, in this case, the defense was planning to pin its hopes on self-defense, or, alternatively, that the shooting was an accident, not on the unlikely, unbelievable proposition that Connie Nicholas did not shoot Forrest Teel. Even without the confession, the circumstantial evidence was nearly overwhelming. Besides, the members of the jury had not claimed that they did not know about the case prior to the trial. They only promised that they could potentially change any opinions they had already formed.

Surely, every one of them knew that she had already confessed, at least to the press from her hospital bed.

So, although the defense would have likely preferred not to have evidence of Connie's confession admitted, in the long run, they felt as though it wouldn't do any more damage than had already been done.

Almost immediately, Detective Smith said that Connie had told him that she had shot him and she wasn't sorry.

"There should be an 'out,'" she told the Detective. "He shoved me. Maybe that's not enough, but I'm not sorry—I loved him, I loved him," Smith reported Connie as saying.

Then, in a strange turn, she reportedly got quiet and told the officer, "You don't shoot someone you love."

He also told Connie that she may face the electric chair for the killing. "I would welcome that. The sooner the better," was her reply.

Finally, the Detective had one more thing to say.

"Connie told me that Mr. Teel had not touched the gun when she fired it at him."

"She also never said it was an accident."

The prosecution celebrated. The defense sat stoically.

The final witness in the prosecution's case was a well-known Indianapolis neurosurgeon, Dr. John Hetherington.

The doctor was a large man with dark, wavy hair and a slightly boyish-looking face that seemed at odds with his 50-plus year-old chronology. He wore a stylish, brown suit and approached the witness stand confidently.

Dr. Hetherington was asked by Jud Haggerty about the injuries to Connie's arms and hands. He, in no uncertain terms, told the court that the most likely cause for Connie's injuries was the pressure of her head resting on them for almost 20 hours as she slipped into a comatose state near the Fall Creek after the shooting. He called it "Saturday Night Paralysis." It is a condition common in people who get so drunk that they pass out, often awkwardly. When an arm or leg is pinned underneath the weight of an unconscious person, the restriction of blood flow will sometimes cause the injury and, in severe cases, even paralysis.

Dr. Heatherington was one of the best. He was well-known and highly respected. His reputation was unassailable. The doctor seemed unshakable in his testimony. His credentials were impressive. He was well-known in Indianapolis and extremely well-respected.

Still, the well-prepared defense team easily deflated the doctor's position.

In a relatively brief cross-examination, Charlie Symmes was able to elicit testimony from the doctor that he had never seen paralysis resulting from a struggle. This seemed to be an odd contention. Certainly paralysis could be the consequence of an injury sustained in a fight.

But the doctor's testimony was virtually neutralized by one simple admission. Dr Hetherington admitted to the younger Symmes on cross-examination that he had neither met nor examined the defendant.

It was a bombshell that destroyed the esteemed doctor's testimony.

With that, on April 12, the prosecution rested its case.

The prosecution ended on a low note. However, over the course of the first week, they had scored several major hits against the defendant. They had presented evidence of the crime, the death, the spacing of the shots, the angle of the bullets in the victim's body, the difficulty in firing the gun and statements from the defendant's own mouth that she was not sorry. Plus, the defendant also had said that Teel had not touched the gun.

The defense was ready. The clever defense lawyers planned to put forth two theories to explain what happened that night in July, 1958. First, they planned to present evidence to show that the shooting was self-defense. Second, they planned to present evidence that the shooting was accidental.

The prosecution knew that the defense was set to launch a two-pronged attack. Prosecutor Bayt found that strategy somewhat incredible and definitely unwise. After all, he pointed out, they couldn't have it both ways. One can't accidentally shoot someone in self-defense. Either she shot Teel in self-defense, or she shot him accidentally. It had to be one or the other and the fact that the defense couldn't make up its mind was a signal to Bayt that they were grasping for a defense.

Connie and her defense team would have an uphill climb.

Frank Symmes announced that Connie Nicholas would be taking the stand as the first defense witness on Wednesday.

During the remaining morning hours of Wednesday, April 7, the court heard various motions as the jury honed its collective Bridge skills. When the judge recessed the proceedings for lunch, he announced that the defense would begin presenting its case after lunch. Word of Connie's impending testimony spread among the town like a tidal wave. Within the one and a half-hour lunch period, the courtroom was jammed, the hallway was nearly impassible and the press area was literally shoulder-to-shoulder. Outside, the gathering throngs obscured the sunlight through the six windows in the old courtroom.

In the previous days of the trial, spectators would come and go during the recesses and breaks. Today, not a single person would leave the courtroom during Connie Nicholas' testimony. During breaks, brown paper bags appeared from purses and shopping bags. The spectators ate their meals in the coveted chairs rather than risk losing their seats to others who mobbed the hallway.

At 2:00 PM, shortly after the judge had entered the courtroom, defense attorney Charlie Symmes rose to his feet at the defense table and announced in his high-pitched voice, "The defense calls Connie Nicholas to the stand."

The 5 foot, 1 inch, 105 pound defendant rose from the chair at the defense table that she had occupied for the last three weeks and nervously, deliberately walked the five steps across the small courtroom, placed her left hand on the soft black cover of the Holy Bible, faced the judge towering over her and swore to tell the truth, the whole truth and nothing but the truth, so help her God.

Dressed in a black suit, her arms caged in the metal braces, she sat gingerly and properly in the uncomfortable wooden witness chair next to the court reporter. She took a deep breath and expelled it quietly as Charlie Symmes moved from his position at the rectangular wooden defense table to examine the defendant.

The courtroom was engulfed in total silence.

By now, the press area to the left of the judge was packed well past comfortable capacity. Reporters and photographers from Life Magazine, the New York Times, The Chicago Tribune battled for space with reporters and photographers from Australia, Japan and England. The biggest event in the world at that moment was occurring in a small, dark basement in downtown Indianapolis.

Although unknown to the jury and spectators, Connie hadn't planned on testifying that day. Her attorneys had told her to be prepared to take the stand the following day after two medical doctors had offered their opinions as to her injuries. Unfortunately, those plans would have to be scrapped when that morning, both doctors had called the defense team to say they had emergencies and could not be in court until the following day.

Trial strategy typically includes ending a case with a bang. Throughout its preparation, the defense had planned to wrap up its case with its star witness, the defendant. With the letdown for the prosecution of Dr. Heatherington's testimony, both the defense and the prosecution would have to end with less.

Since she was not planning on taking the witness stand until the following day, Connie had little time to compose her thoughts before taking her oath. But in a sense, it might have worked out more favorably. Connie had been growing increasingly nervous as her day on the stand approached. Each night, she slept more and more restlessly and for a shorter and shorter time.

The night before, the typical ten-hour-a-night sleeper was down to less than five. Had she been forced to wait another day, she may not have been able to sleep at all, which likely would have affected her testimony and, maybe, even her credibility with the jury.

Symmes began with typical, preliminary questions, such as her name, address, age and occupation. He then launched into the questions that the world had wanted to ask the notorious killer for nine months.

Charlie Symmes opened by asking Connie about her work history, leading her up to the time she took a job at Eli Lilly and Company in 1941. He made sure he took ample time in describing the deaths of her parents, the frequent shuffling during her childhood and her diligent struggle to support herself at a young age.

She told of meeting the handsome Teel within six months of her hiring at Lilly as he would often visit the file room where she worked looking for research material. As an executive, he typically would have had an assistant or a secretary run his errands to the file room. But, after meeting Connie, he always made the trip himself. Almost immediately, he began asking her out.

She didn't dignify his advances, she said. He was married. Simply put, she wasn't interested. Although at the time, Connie wasn't married, she politely refused all of his advances.

It was clear by his attitude and lifestyle that Forrest Teel hadn't heard the word "no" many times in his life. It was also quite clear that he wasn't about to accept it from her.

According to Connie, her rejections of Teel continued for two years. During that time, Connie had been promoted within Lilly and then had moved on to another job with another company, still in downtown Indianapolis. Still, he pursued her. Then, in 1943, the two met completely by chance outside of the Lincoln Hotel in downtown Indianapolis, about a half-mile from Teel's office. They engaged in some polite conversation. He asked her to accompany him into the hotel and have a drink at the bar. She refused. He asked again, she refused again. Finally, he begged her. By now, they were both married, Teel still married to Betty and Connie now married to her first husband, Ray Keifer. For some reason, she relented and agreed to have a drink with him.

By now, Connie was well aware of Teel's reputation as a ladies' man and told the jury that she knew of several other women in his life at the time. Much to the dismay of the audience, Connie didn't name names and Charlie Symmes didn't pursue it further.

The first meeting in the Lincoln Hotel was platonic, but flirtatious. However, it was just days before the two began seeing more of each other. The following Saturday, Teel called Connie's house and asked to come over. Incredibly, Connie said yes. As one reporter put it, at that point, the affair was on. Daily phone calls, secret meetings in hotels, Connie's apartment and even on one occasion, in the fashionable house on Washington Boulevard followed in the ensuing weeks, months and years.

This was no short-term fling for the 29 year-old woman. The more she got to know Forrest Teel, the more Connie became attracted to him. Soon, Connie was in love. She fiercely protected the executive and his family. No one knew of their affair, not even Connie's closest friends.

Forrest would tell her that he loved her as well. She believed it with all her heart.

The defendant, alternately crying, sobbing, and laughing throughout, told the fascinated courtroom of gifts of cash, rent payments, he even paid her car off for her. At one point, he gave her $2,500 in one lump sum, the equivalent of over $18,000 today.

Although her marriage to Ray Keifer had ended during this time, she refused to attribute that event to her increasing fascination with Forrest Teel.

During most of their lengthy love affair, the two were together on average at least twice a week.

On one occasion, Connie had tried to break her addiction to the handsome, successful executive. The reason was understandable. She was getting married again.

During the fifteen year relationship, at times, Connie felt as though she would eventually end up as Mrs. Teel. At still other times, she resigned herself to the realization that there was no future in the relationship. During one period when she was discouraged by her secret romance, she began dating other men. Eventually, she became engaged to Curtis Nicholas. When they were married in October of 1952, she told Forrest Teel that she needed to go on to make a life for herself. She was going to marry again and would not be able to see him anymore.

Teel expressed his displeasure at the impending union, but agreed not to stand in her way. Then, just a few months into Connie's new marriage, the phone rang. Forrest Teel wanted to see her again. Six weeks later, the twice-weekly rendezvous were right back on schedule.

The disproportionately female gallery moaned quietly as she also related a story about their close call in 1955. Curtis traveled in his job and was a performer in local theater. Many nights, even when he was in town, rehearsals provided the opportunity for Connie and Forrest to meet. One particular night Curtis was rehearsing a play at the Civic Theater in Indianapolis. Forrest and Connie were alone in the Nicholas' apartment. Luckily for Connie, they were not in any compromising position at the time.

Curtis came home early, finding Forrest Teel alone in the apartment with his wife.

The quick-thinking Connie, without hesitation, explained that the strange man in the apartment was there to deliver some scotch she had ordered from the liquor store.

According to Connie, Curtis Nicholas bought the unlikely explanation without question.

The following day, Forrest asked Connie if she had had a rough time the night before after he left. She replied that she had.

"Why don't you divorce that crazy son of a bitch?" was his reply.

In March, 1957, Curtis moved out of their apartment at her request.

Early in 1958 Connie requested a divorce from Curtis Nicholas.

She tearfully recounted her last date with Teel in June of 1958. They had celebrated his birthday, a week late, in her apartment in Marcy Village.

About that time, she noticed that he was becoming less available. Their meetings first dwindled to one night per week. Shortly, he began to miss their Thursday night date that had been a weekly staple for over a decade. On the rare occasions he would agree to see her, he would often call and cancel. He refused to make promises. If he was available, he would let her know. The abrupt change in their relationship was upsetting to Connie. Within a few weeks, by the beginning of July, she began to suspect another woman.

In the late Spring of 1958, Connie had moved on to another position. The company for which she was employed as the office manager let her know that they intended to replace its female employees with men. The Equal Employment Opportunity Act was still years away.

At best, they would offer her a lower paying job with less responsibility. She talked this over with Teel, who recommended she quit. As she often did, she took the successful executive's advice.

During the beginning of the summer of 1958, she was staying at home, unemployed and living off the money that Forrest had been giving her. Weeks before she knew that his wandering eye had found a more youthful prey, Connie was becoming all too aware that their relationship was changing. Becoming more despondent with each passing Thursday night and cancelled date, she knew she had to do something. She needed a safety net in case the income she received from Forrest dried up. Connie gave up her "kept" status and began working at the Indianapolis Life Insurance Company.

At about the same time, Connie began taking matters into her own hands.

One night, Connie told the enthralled courtroom, she staked out Teel's office. As he left for the evening, she followed him. A few minutes later, he spotted her distinctive two-tone hardtop in his mirror and sped away. A short chase ensued through the streets of Indianapolis. The power of the Cadillac would normally have been no match for the Chevrolet. However, the area had very few straight roads and he was unable to accelerate long enough to lose her. Once he realized that he was not going to get away from the blue and white Chevrolet, he stopped and confronted her.

During the argument in the street, Connie asked Teel directly if there was another woman. He didn't deny it. "Does she mean anything to you?" she asked. He answered with one word, "No."

But the dressing down from Teel that followed did little to deter the scorned defendant. By sheer chance, she caught up with his white Cadillac later that night about a mile and half north of downtown Indianapolis and followed it to the

Meadowbrook Apartments. Sneaking into the common entryway of the brick apartment building, she copied each of the names that appeared on the mailboxes. Initially, the names meant nothing to her. However, the following day, she looked in a Lilly company directory and found that one of the names she had copied the night before matched. The name was Laura Mowrer, a young secretary at the firm.

In the aftermath of the killing, newspapers around the country reported that Laura and Connie knew each other. In fact, some even reported that they were best friends. Neither was true. They had never even met. But the story was that much more interesting with that detail included.

Still, boldly, Teel would visit Connie's Marcy Village apartment every Saturday. He took a flying lesson in his new plane on Saturday mornings and the weekly commitment provided the perfect cover for their liaisons. Connie continued to let him in.

Teel brazenly continued dating both women for the next several weeks. In response to Connie's objections, he simply told her not to worry. He was "sowing his oats" and would return to her when he got this out of his system.

Shortly after the July 4th holiday in 1958, she was at a stoplight waiting for it to change from red to green. She saw his conspicuous white Cadillac travel through the intersection in front of her. She immediately changed course and caught up with him a few miles away. In the still-moving traffic, she asked him to pull onto a side street. He obliged. She asked him to come over the following Thursday evening, two nights later. She had some recipes she wanted to try.

"I'm busy," was his curt reply.

Still, the busy executive continued to juggle his romances. He continued to call Connie and, although less frequently, continued to visit on Saturday mornings. However, even those minimal contacts were soon discontinued. She saw him one more time on July 17.

She wouldn't see him again until 1:00 AM on July 31.

The evening of July 30 and early morning of July 31, 1958 began quietly but not routinely for Connie. Thursday had been reserved for Forrest for years, yet this Thursday she found herself alone. She didn't like it. She became preoccupied with the thought of her lover with another woman.

To take her mind off him, she visited her neighbors around 5:30, just after dinner. They shared an after-dinner drink and conversation. Connie was depressed and hadn't eaten for days. Her world seemed to be falling apart.

Finally, at about 6:00 PM, she could stand it no longer. She left her apartment and drove the fifteen or twenty minutes to the Meadowbrook Apartments. As she had suspected, the white Cadillac was parallel parked just east of the entrance to Laura Mowrer's building, in the same space as before.

Her suspicions confirmed, she returned home.

Once back in her apartment, Connie began mixing her concoction of pineapple juice and sleeping pills. She counted at least 75 pills in the mixture. The compound was then poured into a pint-sized Thermos that she used for lunches at work during the week.

She opened her purse, and placed the gun inside.

She carefully placed notes around the apartment. She then taped one to the outside of the front door, along with a key to the apartment. One of those notes was entered into evidence and the jury took turns reading it as the trial continued.

> "Dear Forrest:
>
> I know now that we can never go back and mean to one another the things that we have for the past 15 years. Even though you tell me that you still love me, and that this Laura Mowrer means nothing to you and is not the cause of but the result

of our first serious misunderstanding in all these years. Of course, I knew before you did that she was available and would be most cooperative from past conversations and remarks that you told me she had been making. It would seem that knowing all this I still played into her hands. But you see, I too, have a stubborn disposition. Too, she had the advantage of seeing you everyday at the office.

I still love you and even though you are willing to come back I would never have that feeling I have had for the past years in knowing that our love for one another was sincere. There might be another Laura and I just couldn't take it another time. It is most difficult for me to understand how you could turn to her so easily just because she was there and because we had a misunderstanding.

We have never had reason to feel cheap about our love for one another because we both knew that we had a definite goal in 1960-1. Although you have offered me all that Betty has financially that is not what I want or have ever wanted unless I could have you, completely as I have for so many years.

For the first time I can now understand how she became what she is if she truly loved you at one time as I do. However, just for the record, she was already on her way when I first knew you and and there had been others, although you have stated that your attitude with all women other than me had beeen completely negative. Remember, I was the last woman in your life? This I believed and knew this to be true until the past three or four weeks.

I now know fully the suffering and anguish that Curt went through—as I have told you, I was wrong to have married him because I did him a great injustice and he was much too nice a person to be hurt as he was. It was you that wanted me to be so completely yours that caused me to divorce him and as you so recently stated, "That never in your life had one person loved you so completely for yourself as I did." I can now see that you were completely selfish in your love for me and because of this, many innocent people have been hurt.

This has not been written in anger because I am still not angry with you, just hurt and heartbroken and my memories are of the wonderful hours that we did share and the few trips that we did make together. I am sorry that you failed me after all this time.

I now know what I must do and it is something that I have given much thought to, because as I have said before, life without you would have no meaning. My only fear is that I might fail—other than that I have absolutely none. Even though I know it is much easier than seeing you and knowing that I can never again be as completely happy as I have been in the past.

I still love you with all my heart and as you well know there is no halfway point for me when I truly feel as I do about you."

The defense team hoped that the jury would decide that the note was an indication of Connie's predisposition to suicide, but not to murder.

But Charlie Symmes knew he had to deal with the gun. If Connie had merely meant to commit suicide, then why did she take the gun and wait for Forrest Teel in his car for hours? He dealt with it directly, rather than allow the prosecution to bring it up.

"What was your purpose in taking the gun with you?" he asked.

"It was just a thought that if the sleeping medicine did not take effect or do the job that I would use the gun on myself."

From there, Connie left her apartment at approximately 9:00 PM and went to a friend's house. She delivered a sealed envelope to her friend addressed to Curt Nicholas. In it were instructions for the disposition of her body and a check to Curt for $900.00. It also told him how to collect on her life insurance.

She directed him to distribute her ashes over "all of the airfields in Indianapolis."

By 9:15 PM, she was back in her car, heading east to The Meadows once again. She parked her car behind the Phillips 66 service station in a position so that she could see Miss Mowrer's apartment from the windshield of her car. The lights were on in the apartment. The drapes were closed. The Cadillac was still out front.

Slightly after 10:00 PM, Connie started her Chevrolet and left the area. She drove directly back home, then returned to the Meadowbrook Apartments about a half-hour after she had left. She parallel parked against the curb facing east, three or four cars from the white Cadillac. It was now slightly past 10:30 PM.

Neither attorney asked her why she left and went home. That caused some very interesting speculation. Some said she had gone home to get the gun. Some guessed she went to get the bullets. Still others speculated that she was having second thoughts about confronting him. None of these was true.

The truth, told by Connie after the trial, was much less exciting. She had to go to the bathroom and preferred to do so in her own apartment.

Upon her return, Connie left her car and went directly down the line of parked cars to her lover's Cadillac. She checked the front door and found it to be unlocked. Stealthily, she climbed in, shutting the big, heavy door behind her. Just a few feet away from Laura's apartment now, she noticed that the lights were out.

Connie remained semi-prone on the soft, white leather front seat of the luxury car. From her perspective, she could see the windows of Laura's apartment and through the window in the front door of the building, she could see the hallway inside.

Eleven PM passed. Midnight passed. Finally, just before 1:00 AM, she saw the light in the hallway flicker. Someone was coming.

She crouched further down in the car, her eyes just above the bottom of the window. The door to the building opened. Forrest Teel stepped out. There was no turning back now.

Chapter 14

Dear Judge Faulconer:

I want to express my appreciation for your attitude in permitting news photographers to operate in your court. I believe your action and the work of photographers who were assigned to the Connie Nicholas trial provide strong evidence that the presence of photographers does not detract from the dignity of the proceedings nor does it in any way impair the presentation of either the defense or prosecution. On the other hand, the presence of photographers, both still and television, permitted fuller coverage than otherwise would have been possible.

I'm sure all press photographers everywhere appreciate your enlightened attitude.

Letter to Judge Faulconer from the general office of United Press International in New York, 1959

There would be many occasions when the new judge could use help. Unfortunately, with Phil Bayt as the prosecutor on the case, his sources for assistance were as limited as they had ever been in his short career.

However, there was no shortage of unsolicited advice, although the advice he received was certainly of questionable value.

Continually, beginning with the weeks leading up to jury selection, throughout the trial and even in the days following, Judge Faulconer received dozens of letters. Most of these came from well-intentioned court-watchers eager to point, typically, rather obvious things out to the judge.

The correspondence ran the gamut. Some seemed to want only to vent frustration, some made recommendations, for some others, the motive is entirely unclear.

Likewise, the tenor of the letters also covered a wide spectrum. Most were respectful. However, Judge Faulconer received his share of letters questioning his abilities, some in rather disrespectful language.

Some even threatened his life.

Only a few were signed, and of those few, the origin of one letter in particular was especially suspect.

Syracuse, N.Y.
30 March, 1959

Judge Thomas Faulconer,
Indianapolis, Indiana

Dear Judge Faulconer:

About to begin is the murder trial of that sex-crazed you-know-what Connie Nicholas who trailed her paramour for the purpose of putting him out of circulation—a clear-cut case of premeditated murder, if there ever was one—and yet, according to a news item, you have taken, "for study," a minor charge recommendation of her attorneys, which leaves us dumfounded (sic) and wondering what in "ell (sic) kind of a jurist you are, to make so light of the word 'justice.'"

And that's just how such expressions as "getting away with murder" are born, too!

Yours very truly,

Onandaga County Grand Jurors

It is quite doubtful that this letter came from anyone on the Onandaga, New York grand jury. If it did, most certainly, it was without the blessing of the prosecutor of the county who was in charge of the grand jury.

Another sign of its questionable authenticity is the paper upon which it was typed. It was delivered on plain, onionskin typing paper. No letterhead or other identifying marks.

Roughly half of the letters received were in favor of Connie Nicholas going free. These included a handwritten, three page letter signed only, "a friend who reads the papers."

> Judge Faulconer:
>
> Why be so hard on that poor girl who killed her lover? I'd say he deserved everything he got. Only should have been sooner. Before he took 15 years of the girl's life. Then when she gets older he gives her the run around for a younger one. She truly loved him to stay all those years with him...It doesn't mean she's all bad.

Ignoring the obvious application of her logic to Connie's actions, the writer continued:

> ...for one thing because he had money, does that give a person the right to live like a criminal and do all kinds of crooked work and get away with it? Money won't clean his soul or make things right for the life he led that poor woman... Too many men are getting by with just such doings.

The letter was peppered multiple times with the phrase, "Let her go free."

The writer concluded the letter with the sentence, "My best to Connie."

One of the many postcards received came from Springport, Michigan. Dated April 12, 1959, it read:

Hon. Thomas J. Faulconer
Indianapolis, Indiana

I with many others think that Mrs. Connie Nicholas shooting was accidental.

Evidently Forrest Teel used these working girls as his "PUPPETS." Mrs. Nicholas has paid 15 of the best years of her life. I hope she goes free.

The most amazing aspect of the letters defending Connie Nicholas is the lack of consistency in applying these often bewildering standards.

For example, a letter bearing only a postmark from Hobart, Indiana, outlined all of the good qualities the writer purported to see, followed by several references to Laura Mowrer as a tramp—and worse.

Equally represented were those in favor of a harsh punishment for the defendant.

Judge Hon. Faulkner
Criminal Room
Marion County Courthouse
Indianapolis, Ind.

We don't need any woman like Mrs. Nicholas. I am ashamed of that woman. She has hidden tempor (sic). Get rid of her. I like good women and men.

Let your conscious (sic) be your guide.

Good spirit

> [P.S.] Mrs. Nicholas is spending some of the money that Mr. Teel gave her. She is gold digger.

From North Carolina came a handwritten letter. The writer apparently didn't read the news accounts very closely by the number of shots referenced.

> Your Honor,
>
> From such information as given in news accounts of the Nicholas-Teel case one might conclude that Nicholas was a coniving (sic) whore and that Teel was an insatiable whore hopper. And that they were both equally a discredit to decent society.
>
> It also seems unreasonable that a person could shoot another five times with a revolver could be an unintentional accident. It appears more obvious that Nicholas is guilty of deliberate and intentional murder.
>
> I would think it the duty of the court to decent society to discourage marital infidelity or contamination.

The majority of the correspondence also contained biblical references. One anonymous person sent Judge Faulconer 11 pages of handwritten bible verses. No explanation was included and many appear to have no relationship to the case at hand.

From Fort Myers, Florida, a gentlemen wrote of following the case closely and reminded the judge that "One of the Ten Commandments says 'Thou shalt not commit adultery.'" He used this religious quote in an attempt to convince Judge Faulconer that Teel was a very bad person and deserved what he got. The writer completely ignores the fact that Connie was also an adulterer in recommending that she go free.

Some also wrote to the court merely asking for Connie's address.

> Hon. Judge Faulconer
>
> Dear Sir:
>
> With honorable intentions and your approval, we should like to have the mailing address of Connie Nicholas—to write her occassional (sic) "Cheer-up" messages during her next several months of life here.
>
> Confident she'll need friendship, we'd like to help in this, not to sympathize as taking any life is wrong—especially tragically so.

More than a few of the letters were simply incomprehensible. From a letter addressed to the "Men at law and of High Court:"

> ...I'm going to let you in on a little trip that I'm supposed to take to Heaven and to Hell. I say it this way because that is the way the Bible tells us.
>
> There are other worlds and as I start on this tour, I first come to a world where the walls are high and constructed in a way I cannot explain in words, but these will follow the shape of the sky as we would say it. There was no gate.

It was signed, "God Servant."

The letters also had an amusing contingent. A woman in Falls Village, Connecticut carried on an unrequited letter writing campaign to the judge. In her first letter, she simply urged the judge to "do all you can to free Connie Nicholas."

However, in a later letter, she used some astonishing reasoning to support her position.

Judge Thos. J. Faulconer

My dear Judge Faulconer:

Please forgive me for writing again, I felt I simply had to.

I am enclosing a newspaper clipping, which simply startled me. I feel sure you will agree that there is an amazing likeness in Connie's face to our First Lady, Mrs. Eisenhower and surely anyone resembling a good woman such as our Mamie, couldn't possibly be anything but good as well. Please take this into consideration when you advise the jury and help Connie to start a new life, she deserves it. You will never regret it, I am sure.

Some had a distinctly more sinister tone. "Free Connie Nicholas or God will make you suffer," warned a letter from New York. "If she is not released, 3 or 4 jury men will drop dead. This is a prophet talking."

The recommendations and observations crossed racial lines as well. "We colored people are for her," proclaimed one writer. "God bless her, let her live." Any semblance of credibility of this anonymous writer was shattered by his contention that all married men are entitled to seven women. His final paragraph was a demand that the letter be read in open court for everyone to hear, "so the married men can be careful."

The geographic origins of the letters and postcards are a testament to the level of coverage of the case. Letters came from just down the street in Indianapolis and from other towns and cities in Indiana. But they also came from New York, California, Pennsylvania, West Virginia and Florida. All across the country, ordinary people, riveted by what they were hearing, seeing and reading took time from their personal lives to offer their advice, good wishes and predictions to the judge.

Seemingly, some lonesome souls hoped to find a friend in the young judge. "May I tell you—I am the 'Mom' of three nice sons—all grown and married (and one about whom I am greatly concerned)," wrote a woman from Forest Hills, New York. She identified herself by name, followed by her title, "Secretary."

The envelopes and the faces of the postcards were often as interesting as the content. Of the dozens the judge received during the trial, only one contained the street address of the courthouse. A majority of the others were addressed simply to Thomas J. Faulconer, Indianapolis, Indiana. They contained no street address. Zip codes were not yet used.

Some become quite creative in their addresses. One, addressed:"To the jury and judge of Connie Nicholas Court" began with the salutation, "Men of Law."

In a scene reminiscent of *Miracle on 34th Street*, despite the incomplete addresses, the diligent postal service delivered them all to the judge at the Marion County Courthouse. Provided the 6 cents postage was affixed.

The envelope "To Judge Faulconer, Main Court, Indianapolis, Indiana, In charge of Nicholas and Teel" was delivered accurately. Even a postcard addressed only to "Indianapolis, Indiana" found its way to the judge's chambers, the postal workers apparently reading the note on the back to decide to deliver it to the ancient courthouse.

Most likely, the judge would not have been swayed in either direction by these letters. However, that proposition will never be proven. The letters were opened by court personnel and placed in a file.

Judge Faulconer never read them.

He still hasn't.

Chapter 15

"I knew things were going too smoothly. Something had to happen."
Judge Thomas J. Faulconer
April 7, 1959

By now, Judge Faulconer was finally settling into his role as elected ringmaster of his judicial circus. For the past several days, the objections that had been raised had been routine, the rules he had promulgated for the media were working without interruption and even with Connie on the stand, things seemed to be progressing smoothly.

Unfortunately for the judge, his next problem would be one that he couldn't have predicted in a million years. In fact, when Frank Symmes heard about it, he was quoted as saying he had never heard of anything like that in his 40 years of practicing law.

Despite his weeks of preparation, there was no way the judge could have seen this coming.

Within 24 hours, the Connie Nicholas case would involve the governor, both political parties, the state attorney general and a widow who had just lost her husband the day before.

Papers across the country printed stories about the trial of the infamous murderess, Connie Nicholas. Many had printed so many stories about her that they simply referred to her in headlines as "Connie." No further description was necessary. Connie's name was becoming synonymous with jilted mistresses who kill. Indeed, by now, with diminutive Connie on the stand, the story was routinely making its way across the oceans and into the newspapers of other countries on other continents.

But a story in the Indianapolis newspapers on April 8, 1959, would cause the wheels of justice to grind to a halt.

County Clerk is typically a position that receives little attention at election time. In the election of 1958 in Marion County, the public had many, much more exciting races to watch. Former Mayor Bayt was running for prosecutor and a U.S. Senate race was up for grabs as well. Virtually no one even noticed that Democrat Harry Gasper and Republican Ed McClure were fighting for the same office as Marion County Clerk.

In the Democrat sweep of 1958, Harry Gasper had defeated his Republican opponent by just under 10,000 votes in a race that saw over 220,000 cast. In January, 1959, Gasper was sworn in as Marion County Clerk.

He would hold the job for only slightly over three months.

Harry Gasper was only on the job a short time before entering the hospital. Late in the day on April 7, 1959, Harry Gasper was dead.

The Indianapolis Star, the morning paper in central Indiana, still covered the Connie Nicholas trial with the fervor and thoroughness that trial watchers had become accustomed to over the previous weeks. In 10 point type, a verbatim transcript of Connie's testimony from the day before covered almost two entire pages, displaced only by a department store advertisement.

The Connie Nicholas story shared the front page with the story of Harry Gasper's death. However, the newspaper, like most everyone in Indianapolis, made no connection between the two events so early in the day.

Judge Faulconer and the six lawyers involved in the Connie Nicholas case made the connection immediately.

Judge Faulconer took the bench at his usual time, 9:30 AM, on Wednesday, April 8, just long enough to tell the assembled crowd of spectators, press and court personnel that the trial would be recessed until the following day.

Disappointed spectators would not see any testimony on this day. The jurors would get the day off.

While the clerk's office was one of lesser importance in the eyes of the electorate, the truth was, it was very important to the court system. The Indiana Constitution requires that all court proceedings be certified by the appropriate clerk. Courts at the state level, such as the appellate and supreme courts in Indiana needed to be certified by the state clerk of courts. Proceedings at the county level, such as the trial in Judge Faulconer's court required certification by the Marion County clerk. The law contained a provision outlining the proper procedure in the illness or absence of a clerk. In that circumstance, the deputy clerks, of which there was one per court, could certify proceedings on behalf of the elected clerk. However, the law contained no guidance in the event of the death of the clerk.

Without a county clerk, there was serious doubt among the judge and the lawyers whether this trial could even continue.

At the time, the Governor of Indiana was Harold Handley, a Republican. For a short time, it appeared that the issue of the vacant clerk's office would be resolved very quickly. During the day on April 8, while the trial was in recess, the governor simply appointed a clerk to the position.

By taking such initiative and naming a clerk for a county, the governor caused objection on two fronts. First, the powers in Marion County, the County Commissioners, became incensed that their power to run the county had been usurped. They believed the governor had every right to appoint a vacancy at the state level, but the power to appoint a new clerk for the county belonged to them. Second, many people became suspicious and, in some cases, outraged, with the governor's choice for Marion County clerk.

Governor Handley named Edwin McClure, the Republican who had been beaten by Democrat Gasper for that very office months before.

The Indiana Attorney General immediately sanctioned the selection, opining that McClure would serve the remainder of Gasper's term and would, therefore, be up for reelection in 1962.

McClure further stirred the tempest by assembling the staff that had been selected by the deceased Gasper and appointing them as his own staff, followed by his announcement that he would begin the "orderly" replacement of the Democrat staff with Republicans.

Other officials didn't quite see things with the same clarity as the governor and the attorney general.

Miffed by the appointment of a Republican to fill the spot held by their Democrat boss, the two chief deputy clerks immediately walked off the job.

Believing that the deceased Democrat should have been replaced by their action, the Marion County Commissioners, surprisingly comprised of two Republicans and one Democrat, issued their own opinion that the selection and appointment of the new county clerk should fall to them.

Another reason for the political tension caused by the death of Mr. Gasper lay deeper. The county clerk's position also included an automatic appointment to the county election board. The three-member board was comprised at the time of two Democrats and one Republican. The loss of one Democrat and the replacement with a Republican member would reverse the majority of the committee. The result would be the ultimate dismissal of 65 Democratic clerk's office employees and the unseating of 10 Democrat members of the county election board. They would all be replaced with Republicans.

It would be quite a political coup for the governor in the most populous county in the state.

Criminal Court #2 was certainly not the only court whose proceedings were interrupted by Gasper's death and the resultant tug-o-war. Some courts continued with business as usual. Some locked their doors and everyone went home pending the outcome. Still others tried as best they could to work within the law given the unusual situation. In Municipal Court, which tried smaller criminal cases, Judge Charles Dougherty began summarily continuing cases which had been filed the day before or earlier since proceedings against them would not be valid without a clerk to certify the record. Those that had charges filed against them after the death of Gasper on April 8 celebrated as those charges were dismissed by the judge. One defendant promised the judge that he would be at home and cooperative when the police came to arrest him again after the political questions were resolved. As the defendants exited the courtroom, many were immediately re-arrested and held until the clerk squabble was over and new charges could be filed.

Judge Faulconer spent the morning huddling with the lawyers in the case, attempting to find a solution to the problem caused by the clerk's death. The result was several different opinions, but no clear authority which pointed to a resolution.

The judge contacted the Indiana Attorney General's office and asked for a legal opinion. In a questionable grasp of the situation, a deputy attorney general told the judge, without any research, that the trial could continue without interruption.

However, the judge and the attorneys agreed unanimously to recess the trial until a more satisfactory answer could be obtained.

If the trial continued, and was found invalid due to the lack of a county clerk, Judge Faulconer would be required to hear the entire case again, from jury selection on. Four months would have been wasted. No one wanted that.

The following day, the Marion County Commissioners met, or, more precisely, a quorum, met, selected and appointed their own county clerk. One of the Republican members attended the meeting along with the sole Democrat member. The other Republican refused to attend.

The Commissioners selected the widow of the late clerk, Harry Gasper, Louise Gasper.

For the next day, Marion County had two clerks, although determining which was more entitled to the position was a difficult task.

By now, Judge Faulconer believed that he had arrived at a solution to the dilemma that faced the court. The following morning, he made an official entry into the docket book of the court.

"To avoid any question of technical qualification of Mr. McClure, I am using my inherent power to appoint a clerk of this court, if necessary. Therefore, I am appointing Mr. McClure clerk pro tem of this court."

In retrospect, the choice of Mr. McClure over Mrs. Gasper was a surprising one. Mrs. Gasper was a Democrat as was Judge Faulconer. Mr. McClure was a Republican. The young judge could have potentially scored politically by agreeing that the Democrat had more right to the job. For whatever reason, he didn't.

Shortly after 9:30 AM, the defendant was returned to the courtroom and her handcuffs were removed by the jail matron. The spectators' seats were nearly empty, all but the most die-hard spectators having tired of waiting through the extended period of inaction.

The jury was seated once again in the jury box.

The trial soon continued. Connie Nicholas was called once again to the stand and her direct examination by Charlie Symmes continued.

For 14 minutes.

After just 14 minutes of testimony, Judge Faulconer was handed a message by his bailiff, Fred Titus. Judge Faulconer read it in disbelief.

The secretary of state, a Democrat, had refused to certify the appointment of McClure as clerk. Without the signature of the secretary of state, even the recognition in the official court record was of no consequence.

Once again, legally, at least arguably, the clerk's office was vacant.

The judge interrupted the testimony of the defendant and announced that the court was once again in recess, his gavel bearing the brunt of his frustration.

He stormed from the bench, his black robe flowing behind him, barreled into his chambers, drew a cigar from his inside coat pocket, ripped it from the cellophane wrapper and jammed it into his mouth. He then forcefully hung his robe from a hook on the coat rack, paced in front of his desk momentarily and stormed from the courthouse.

No one knew how long this political standoff could last, least of all Judge Faulconer. The judge walked the downtown Indianapolis area stewing, steaming and searching for a solution. He once again, talked the dilemma over with some of the older, more experienced attorneys in town. The press and the few spectators remaining were still gathered in the courtroom. No one knew that the judge had left.

After about an hour of roaming the downtown streets, it came to him.

The power of a judge is awesome. Although subject to review by a higher court at a later date, a judge can have a defendant released, have an attorney held in contempt or even have someone arrested, all on his word.

He can even appoint a clerk for his court.

Judge Faulconer knew now he didn't have the power to appoint a clerk for the entire county. The secretary of state had just taught him that lesson. But he did have the power, he concluded, to appoint a clerk for his tiny courtroom. And since his clerk was still, technically, a duly sworn and appointed deputy clerk, having been so sworn by ex-clerk Gasper and having not been removed from her position, he appointed her and swore her in as the official court clerk of Marion County Criminal Court #2.

All parties agreed with his action and, finally, the trial continued.

Just before noon, the judge once again entered the courtroom and took his place behind the bench. He explained the situation to the attorneys and spectators and called the lunch recess.

By 2:00 PM, the court was back in session, Connie had been returned to the courtroom from her holding cell, her handcuffs had been removed. The jury was led back into the jury box.

Unfortunately, the quick reconvention of the trial caught many hopeful spectators by surprise. Only 20 of the 50 seats were filled when the doors to the courtroom were ordered shut until another recess was called. Hundreds of disgruntled citizens complained about missing their chance to watch Connie Nicholas testify. They became more vocal when it was discovered that the large keyholes in the doors had been covered. Eventually, the crowd discovered a tiny scratch in the frosting of the glass framed in the doors to the courtroom and took turns peeking through it.

The bombshells were coming one after another. But Judge Faulconer had just dodged the biggest one yet.

At times it seemed as though all of Indianapolis was either in the tiny courtroom, waiting in the hallway or taking a turn at one of the six courtroom windows. It became the predominant topic of conversation across fences, at Betty Brite Laundromats and water coolers across the country. But not everyone wanted to participate in the speculation and rumor mongering that surrounded the famous case.

Betty Teel, the wife of the slain executive, refused to attend the trial. Shortly before the beginning of jury selection, she and her son, Tommy, left their home in Indianapolis and traveled to Texas to stay with relatives for a short time. They made every attempt to avoid the scandalous coverage. The worldwide coverage made that difficult if not impossible.

Betty did tell the police that she had no inkling of her husband's infidelity. This contention seems highly unlikely, however. Those close to Teel, including Connie Nicholas, claimed that the dashing executive in fact had many girlfriends in the time prior to meeting Connie Nicholas. Even Connie expressed her disbelief on the record that Betty could have possibly been oblivious to Forrest's lifestyle.

In addition to her interviews with police, Betty did make one public statement during the trial. It was the only time she would speak publicly about the murder of her husband of 26 years. She professed total faith in the legal system. She was certain the jury would do exactly what they would be charged to do.

Asked about her activities, plans and thoughts on the trial, her statement, offered through her attorney, read:

"There couldn't be much news in my breakfast and dinner dishes or in cooking for Tommy's good healthy appetite. That, with my parent-school activities and a women's club or two wedged in between, is my full-time job.

"My plans? I have no plans beyond Tommy's education and my homemaking. We intend to do that here in Indianapolis. It's our hometown and we both have many good friends of long-standing.

"Along with about everyone, it seems I've been having a bout with a real stubborn 'flu bug.' I think I may have it under control. Time will tell.

"Trial? I have been taught to have faith in the processes of justice. That is the special and proper business for the courts and juries and not for my newspaper comment. The result, I am sure, will be the jury's good conscience view of the actual evidence and of the laws that protect the lives of the citizens and safeguard the institutions of the community."

She also denied ever knowing anything about Forrest's girlfriends and affairs.

Both the interviews with police and the statement issued by Mrs. Teel were much more revealing than they appeared at first blush. They demonstrate one common element that both Forrest and Betty had in their marriage, perhaps the one thing that kept them together for all those years. Form was more important than substance.

Throughout the marriage, the Teel's labored to keep the illusion of their happy union intact. They lived in the right house, belonged to the right club, knew the right people. They attended society functions together, always the picture of happiness and wealth. They would attend open houses at their son's school regularly. According to schoolmates and teachers, a more loving, happy couple did not exist.

The Teel's routinely redecorated their Washington Boulevard home. The house was always fashionable and clean. No toys littered the driveway, the bushes were trimmed and the lawn cut. By outward appearances, the Teel's were the perfect family.

But that was the point—by outward appearances.

Beneath the shiny veneer was a relationship that had been rotting for most of the years it existed.

The Teels had no "close" friends as a couple. Forrest had his friends. Betty had her friends. Forrest's social friends were mainly his golfing partners and a few men from work. He was careful to keep his extracurricular activities from them. Betty's friends were often from the neighborhood, although she did have a few that she had met through Lilly functions and parties.

Tragically, virtually all of her friends had one thing in common. They felt sorry for her. And many of them didn't care for her husband.

Despite Connie's assertions under oath, Forrest Teel was not a violent man. There is no evidence that he ever struck either Betty or Tommy. However, he could make Betty's life miserable in other ways.

According to acquaintances, when the two were together in their home, behind the closed doors and away from the general public eye, from Forrest's perspective, Betty could do nothing right. She was expected to be a servant, comforting and waiting on her husband while asking no questions about his work or social life.

Betty's friends told of treatment at the hands of her husband coldly calculated to degrade, dominate and humiliate the loyal wife.

In 1980 or 1990, perhaps Betty might have left the successful executive. But in 1950, that was not such an easy option.

Besides, divorce would spoil the image for both.

A smoker for years, Betty began chain smoking, a nervous habit designed to calm her fraying nerves.

Eventually, probably in the earlier years of their marriage, Betty found another way to cope with the difficult home life she had built for herself. Hard liquor became her best friend.

Betty reportedly drank to intoxication most days. As her problems continued and escalated, and her tolerance to the alcohol increased, so did her consumption. She was a small woman, but was ingesting a larger and larger quantity as time progressed.

Forrest didn't seem to care. The cost of the liquor was certainly no concern. They had plenty of money from his exorbitant salary. As long as the false front the two had so carefully crafted remained intact, Betty's drinking was a small price to pay. Indeed, he may have even seen opportunity in her drinking. Her frequent binges and the required recoveries allowed him to carry on his affairs with little suspicion or questioning from his wife. In addition, he may have viewed her drinking as his justification should he ever decide to divorce her.

As Betty's drinking increased, her parenting skills decreased. She spent less and less time with Tommy and more and more time on the couch or in bed. Eventually, her drinking took its toll on Tommy. Neighbors and friends reported that he became more and more spoiled and resentful. He became, what one family friend called, "a first-class brat." In short, he became less like his mother and more like his father.

In reality, Forrest took a life in his own right. Betty was, by all accounts, a bright, pleasant woman, committed to her family more than herself. But Forrest's hedonistic behavior changed all that. Her friends tried repeatedly to include her in other pursuits and to invite her over to get away from him. But, for whatever reason, Forrest came first.

The public was disappointed in Betty's tight-lipped manner in the wake of the murder. The gossip-hungry nation wanted to hear all sides of the tragedy, including the perspective of the widow. They wanted to hear about their relationship, why she married such a man, why she didn't divorce him, what their life was like.

The public would remain disappointed and, in a few months, shocked.

Connie's direct testimony continued, conducted artfully by defense attorney Charlie Symmes.

Reminded of her testimony just before the last recess by the court reporter, Connie quietly continued. Teel had just exited the apartment building where Laura Mowrer lived.

Connie related how Teel strode directly to the driver's door of the car, on the opposite side from the apartment building. Upon opening the door, he immediately saw Connie. However, Teel maintained his composure, not acknowledging her until he was inside the car and the light was out. The calculating Teel was still thinking. He didn't want to upset his burgeoning relationship with Laura.

Once the two were inside the car, he asked her what she was doing there. Simultaneously, he started the engine and put the car in drive. Again, he was concerned about things continuing to look normal to Laura.

The hours of suppressed emotion and increasing anger sprayed from Connie like a geyser. "I have spent 15 years protecting you and Tommy and now you are out in public about Laura Mower. Being parked there, you might as well have been parked on Monument Circle. You might as well have taken her to the country club," an understandably upset Connie told him.

The couple continued driving north on Meadows Drive to just south of 39th Street.

"I know you have been to Washington or New York with her last week!" The pent up anger poured from Connie's mouth.

Finally, Teel had had enough. He stopped the car and ordered her out. "This is none of your business. Get out and don't bother me anymore!" he commanded.

"Go ahead," Charlie Symmes urged, as the courtroom literally hung on her every word. Jurors, spectators and court employees alike were leaning forward anxiously awaiting the next chapter in her story.

"All of a sudden, he hit me on the right side of the face. And as he hit me, threw me and shoved me across the seat of the car. I told him 'you won't have to worry about me any longer. I won't be around.'"

"I put my hand on the gun," she said.

"What was your purpose in taking the gun with you?" Charlie Symmes asked.

"Objection!" Thomason yelled.

More quietly, he explained, "To allow the defendant to answer that question would be to invite perjury and untruth."

That was, at least, a creative objection. The prosecution team knew the answer Connie would give and they wanted to keep her from opening her mouth. Connie was about to say that she brought the gun to commit suicide.

To maintain that a defendant cannot testify because it may be untrue was ludicrous.

In reality, Thomason knew that his objection would be overruled.

It was.

"It was just a thought that if the sleeping medicine did not take effect or do the job that I would use the gun on myself."

Connie continued to rivet the courtroom with her explanation of her actions that fateful night. After Teel had shoved her, she had pulled the gun from her purse, and said, "You won't have to worry about me any longer. I won't be around." According to Connie, she then put the gun to her head.

Teel lunged at the gun, saying, "Don't be a damned fool!" He grabbed her right arm.

The gun went off.

"He continued holding onto my arm. My shoulder began to pain and I felt a crack in my upper arm. I was trying to get away from him. Finally, he let go of my arm. I got out of the car, walked north on 39th Street."

"Do you know how many shots were fired?"

"I knew that one shot was fired. That is when he grabbed my arm. I have been told since there were three shots."

"What did you do then?"

"I walked back a few steps on 39th, then looked back. I saw Mr. Teel lean over and close the car door. The car was in motion. I started toward the north. I continued to my car and drove from there to the same exit from 39th and 38th, headed west again from 38th.

"During the time the shots were fired did Mr. Teel say anything?

"We were struggling over the gun."

"Did you know he had been hit?"

"I did not know Mr. Teel had been hit. I would not have left him," the tearful Connie testified.

She continued, "As I passed Meadows Drive over my right shoulder I saw his car in the drive of the Phillips station. It was in motion. I thought I was being followed by him. I went east and on the first through-street headed north I believe it was Millersville (Road) to 46th, then left and went over an embankment and came to the place where I was found in my car."

Connie then related how her car had become mired in the mud, made worse by the rain that had begun shortly after the shooting that night. She looked around the interior of the car and found a shopping bag. She opened the passenger door and climbed out, placing the shopping bag under the rear wheel hoping to gain enough traction to drive out of the mud.

It didn't work.

She climbed back into the car, having left the door open. Once inside, she locked the door, took the cap off the lethal mix of pineapple juice and sleeping pills and drank the paste-like substance.

Her already nervous stomach couldn't tolerate the mixture. Almost immediately, Connie felt as though she would vomit. She unlocked the door and climbed from the car. No sooner had she alit from the car, she became ill in the grass and mud. Somewhat dazed, she climbed back in the car and closed the door, failing to lock it this time. She checked the Thermos that contained the suicide potion and found that some was left. She then ingested that as well.

The next memory she had was awakening days later in General Hospital.

The disoriented Connie originally thought she was waking up in her apartment. A female office worker from the Indianapolis Police Department was in her room and told her that she had shot Forrest Teel.

Before resting his examination of the star witness, Charlie Symmes took the opportunity to reinforce with the men of the jury the extent of Connie's injuries.

"Would you state to the jury the condition of your right arm?"

"My shoulder and upper right arm were paining very severely. I couldn't move the arm."

"Let me ask you this. What was the condition of your arm before July 31?"

"I have always had perfect health and never had any trouble with my arms or hands.

"You may cross examine."

Judge Faulconer looked at the clock and recessed the trial for the day.

Francis Thomason was salivating like one of Pavlov's dogs. He couldn't wait to get his turn to tell what, according to the prosecution, really happened.

Chapter 16

"Why don't you investigate why the county clerk died? It could be another murder, to produce this situation to get her free to murder again. I bet he turned her down."
Letter to Judge Faulconer,
April, 1958

Thomason had rightfully earned the position of Chief Trial Deputy for the Marion County Prosecutor's office. He had courtroom experience that spanned many years in Indiana. He was a lifelong government servant who liked nothing more than "nailing the bad guy." He was a cop's prosecutor.

He was also smart. In fact, some called him the "professor" for his ability to comprehend issues in the law. He had taught some of Indiana's best defense lawyers their craft.

When court convened at 9:30 AM on Friday, April 11, Thomason went right to work. His demeanor set the tone immediately. He didn't like Connie Nicholas and he thought she was a liar.

He saw it as his job to prove it.

He began with some "jabs," short questions requiring short answers that, mainly, recounted some of the harmless details of her earlier testimony. He asked about where she parked when she got to Laura's apartment. He asked about the distance between her car and Teel's Cadillac.

He then asked an open-ended question. Speaking of the location near Fall Creek where Connie was found, he asked, "What happened there?"

"I pulled up thinking I was still being followed by Mr. Teel. I saw a car come off Fall Creek (Road) over the hill and turn off the lights. I became more frightened, took the paper bag and put it under the wheels of my car, but I was mired in the mud and could not move."

Thomason appeared very interested, not nearly as confrontational, much more inquisitive.

"What was the condition of the ground there at that time?"

"It had been raining. It was wet enough that my car was mired down."

That is what the wily veteran wanted to hear.

"You got out and then you got back in, is that right?"

"Yes."

"After taking the compound you became ill?"

"Yes."

"How soon?"

"Almost immediately."

"And you vomited?"

"I got out of the car and I did vomit."

"Which side did you get out?"

"The right side."

Thomason produced a picture, handing it to the defendant. The picture was a black and white 8x10 glossy, taken by a newspaper reporter at the scene when her car was found. Connie was unconscious in the front seat and one of the police detectives was climbing in next to her.

"I will ask you observe your shoes," Thomason said as he walked confidently from the witness stand for effect.

Nearing the jury, he asked, "Do you see any mud on those shoes?"

"I can't see the soles," she replied.

Changing tacks, Thomason then asked, "You testified in reference to the condition of your right arm. Will you describe to the jury the condition of that arm as you approached 49th and Fall Creek?"

"I just know that my arm was in great pain."

"Were you able to move it?"

"I am a little vague about that. I was able to drive my car."

"I didn't ask you that," came the terse reply. "I asked you whether you were able to move your arm."

"I moved my arm so far as I know."

"Did you drive your car?"

"Yes."

"Did you drive in a manner you normally drive your car?" Was there anything unusual about the way you drove the car?"

"I may have been using my left arm more than my right."

"You say you had a Thermos bottle with you?

"Yes, in my car."

"Does it have a top on it?"

"It had a stopper in the bottle with a cap on it."

"Did you take that cap off?"

"As I remember I did."

"Do you recall what hand you took it off with?"

"I do not remember, but I took the cap off."

"Are you right handed?"

"Yes."

The prosecution hoped that the jury would understand the line of questioning. If Connie's arm had been injured in the struggle with Teel as she maintained, how could she drive her car, then open the top on the Thermos?

Later, Thomason turned to the little gun used to kill Teel.

He questioned her repeatedly about the size of the gun, the difference between that gun and the first one she had considered. All she would say is that she knew nothing about guns. To her, a gun was a gun.

She had purchased 12 bullets with the gun. However, she had never loaded it. Gano, the man who sold it to her, had loaded it for her.

Thomason asked why the safety wasn't on if she didn't intend to use the gun with Teel.

Connie played dumb again. She said she didn't know how it worked.

Thomason then went for the jugular. He forced Connie to re-examine virtually every detail of the killing.

"Did you take the [Thermos] jug with you to his car?"

"No."

"After he came over to the car, what did he say to you?"

"He opened the car and wanted to know what I was doing there. First, he started to drive away and then wanted to know what I was doing there. I said I came to talk to him. He immediately started to drive away. He drove east on 39th Street, then south and then west on 38th Street."

"Where did you go from there?"

"We came back on Meadows Drive, south of 39th Street."

"Is that where you got out of the car?"

"That is right."

"Were you sitting in the car at that time?"

"I was sitting to the right of the driver's seat."

"How wide is the front seat?"

"I do not know."

"Is it wide enough for three people?"

"Yes, I think so. I was sitting to Mr. Teel's right. I was not too close to the door. Mr. Teel was driving."

Thomason was hoping to convey to the jury the unlikelihood that Teel would have been able to lunge at that gun and grab it without Connie seeing it coming.

"Was he facing forward when driving?"

"Yes."

Thomason had scored another point. If Teel had been facing forward, he couldn't easily have reached across the large car and grabbed Connie's right arm, the arm that was closest to the opposite window.

"At the time that he struck you, where were you sitting then."

"Just to his right."

"What did he strike you with?"

"I do not know, I was hit in the face."

"Were you looking at him at the time?"

"Yes. It happened so fast."

"Then what happened?"

"I took the gun from my purse."

"Where was the purse?"

"In my lap."

"Was it open?"

"I opened my purse after I was struck."

"What was said after he struck you?" he asked.

"He pushed me to one side and said, 'Do not follow me anymore.' I ended up next to the door."

"Did you make a movement with the gun?"

"Yes."

"After you made a movement, did Mr. Teel make any movements?"

"Yes. He grabbed my arm."

Connie went on to explain that she didn't remember if she was facing forward and that the more upset Teel got with her, the closer he moved to her in the car.

She still recalled only one shot.

She also claimed that he continued to clench and twist her right arm even after the first shot.

From there, Thomason changed course asking about the Teel's son.

"Did you know his son? Had you ever met him?" adopting a more conversational tone.

"Yes, sir. His *adopted* son," she replied.

"How old was he when you met him?"

"You mean the son?"

"Yes. How old was the son?"

"About 2 ½ or 3 when I first met him, I guess."

"How frequently did you see the boy?"

"On occasional Saturday afternoons," she answered calmly.

Thomason knew he had scored big. He waited, casually strolling toward the jury as the answer registered with those in the court.

Connie had just admitted that Teel had brought his young son with him on dates with his mistress.

"Have you given any thought to the effect that would have on his child?" he asked.

"I saw no harm in Mr. Teel's bringing the boy to the apartment," she answered.

The courtroom was stunned by this low-key line of questioning.

After just a few more questions, during which Connie told how she had typed one of her suicide letters prior to learning the name of Laura Mowrer, then inserted the name later when retyping the letter, Connie stepped down from the witness stand and court adjourned for the weekend.

On Monday, in an anticlimactic end to the testimony, the defense called two doctors who had examined Connie's arms. Neither doctor was as well-known or as well respected as Dr. Heatherington, but they had personally examined Connie and, frankly, their testimony was more credible. Dr. Heatherington had lost much of his credibility when he testified that he had never seen nerve damage from wrenching of an arm. Even the laypersons on the jury had a tough time swallowing that.

Court would reconvene on Tuesday at 9:30 AM for what was expected to be the final day of the Connie Nicholas trial.

Chapter 17

"Connie Prays, Awaiting Jury Action"
Chicago Sun-Times
April 15, 1959

The weather had proved as unpredictable as the action in the courtroom during the month the trial had been conducted. The cold weather in mid-March had given way to a pre-summer heat wave during much of the proceedings. The partial basement that housed Criminal Court #2 was neither built nor ventilated properly for its present use. Steam pipes feebly camouflaged with paint that matched the walls in the courtroom ran up the wall directly behind the jury.

At one point, the pipes began clanging loudly prompting the judge to announce, on the record, that they were under attack.

Years later, when asked to describe the courtroom, one juror would sum his recollection in one word: hot.

Luckily, by the end of the trial in mid-April, the heat wave had broken and temperatures had returned to the 60s, much more seasonal for the Midwest in April.

Before final arguments could be presented to the jury, the court had to decide on the instructions it would give to the jury. Each side presented its suggested instructions, predictably skewed to provide a favorable verdict. The court also had its own instructions, but would defer to one submitted by the attorneys if convinced to do so.

The legal wrangling over the instructions took place outside the hearing of the jury who were, once again, engrossed in game after game of Bridge in the jury room under the watchful eye of the court bailiffs. The arguments took a full day. Although the hearing on instructions was open to the public, those that made the trek to the downtown courthouse were disappointed as the day's activities were much more technical than anyone could find interesting.

Finally, with the instructions settled by the judge, always to the dismay of the attorneys who idealistically hope that the judge will adopt those submitted without modification, final arguments were set to begin.

Judge Faulconer allowed one and one-half hours for each side to present its final argument.

Like so many courtroom procedures, final arguments are not typically as they are portrayed on television and in the movies. While for entertainment value, final arguments are impassioned pleas made first by the prosecution, then by the defense, in reality, the progression begins with the prosecution, followed by the defense, and concluded by the prosecution once again.

The judge typically allocates a total time to each side. Each side can use it as it sees fit. In other words, if, as in the Connie Nicholas trial, each side has one and one-half hours, the prosecution can use one-half hour at the beginning followed by one hour at the end or any other combination it sees advantageous.

Likewise, television dramas tend to show one attorney handling the final argument. In truth, each attorney on the defense team or prosecution team may present a portion of the closing plea.

The final argument phase of Connie Nicholas' trial started with the impressive young Deputy Prosecutor Haggerty methodically pointing out the discrepancies in Connie's version of the facts to the men on the jury.

There was no mud on her shoes. There was no evidence she had exited the car and vomited. There was no reason to think that Teel would be violent. There was no reason for her to drive across town to get a gun.

"She sought out Forrest Teel. She had no reason to expect that she would have to defend herself. She voluntarily lay in wait for him and provoked an argument. If she was struck on the hard, thick skullbone with such great strength as she says, why were there no bruises on Teel's hands? Why did she not react as any woman would, and either strike back or scratch?"

"No," he continued, "she did not seek to use her hands. She went straight for the gun, nestling in the purse on her lap, undisturbed by this 'violent' struggle, the safety off, all ready to fire."

Haggerty concluded his opening salvo, turning to face Connie Nicholas. Looking her straight in the eye, unwavering, he calmly told the jury, "There was another trial on July 31, 1958. Unlike this trial, that one lasted three to four hours. And the only other witness to what happened in that car is absent. He will never be here. That absent witness was executed."

Raising his voice, Haggerty pointed directly at Connie and said, "His executioner sits right here. There is the judge, jury and executioner of Forrest Teel."

Connie began to cry.

As Jud Haggerty took his seat at the prosecution table, Joe Quill rose to his feet for the defense. His job was to convince the jury of Connie's integrity, to convince them her story was the truth.

"I have come to the conclusion that Connie Nicholas has told no falsehood. Her defense is based on her story of what happened that evening."

"She pulled the gun and said she meant to shoot herself. He grabbed her arm and twisted it until it cracked. How long was she to take this punishment?" he asked.

Quietly, he added, "Yes, the gun was there. But her purpose was suicide, not murder."

Joe Quill then handed the final argument reigns to Charlie Symmes.

Charlie Symmes hammered home many of the points that Joe Quill had made. However, he wanted to make it clear that the defense was not in any way condoning the 15-year illicit relationship. But, "if it is vindictiveness for which the state prosecutes, we can herewith hand them a present of 8 ½ months in prison, a broken life, and a body twisted and broken forever."

It was a clever ploy. First, Quill was telling the jury that, personally, he didn't think she did it. Second, according to Symmes, even if she did, she has paid her debt with her prison time, albeit in a hospital, and her injuries.

Chief Deputy Prosecutor Thomason pushed his chair from the prosecution table.

Thomason, normally monotone, studious and professorial, became melodramatic, invoking the bible, among other tactics.

"She left him to die," were his first words to the jury, spoken quietly and evenly.

After a significant pause, he continued. "In that first hour of July 31, 1958, she stood there a murderess. And when she was asked, 'Where is Abel?' she said, and as repeated over and over again, 'I know not. I am not my brother's keeper.'"

According to Thomason, Connie was trying every defense she could find. She tried to get the jury's sympathy with stories of suicide. She tried to explain it away as an accident. She said it was self-defense. The injuries were simply a red herring, he said, a distraction to cloud the real issue.

And what was her motive, he concluded? "There was just one. This was a jealous woman. And in his final judgment, may God have mercy on her soul."

During the final arguments, the defense put great emphasis on the letters and notes that Connie had left outlining her pending death and providing instructions for her body and property. Clearly, they argued, this was a woman planning on killing herself. This explained the purchase of the gun and the fact that she had it with her on that night.

Perhaps, though, according to the prosecution, this explanation was too simple. Given that Connie had weeks to plot her crime, isn't is possible she conveniently crafted those notes as part of a defense strategy, just in case she was caught, arrested and tried? Besides, if Connie bought the gun to kill herself, why did she drive all the way to the other side of town? Who would have cared where the gun came from if she had used it on herself?

Further, the prosecution team pointed out, it only takes one bullet to commit suicide. Why was she carrying twelve? And, if she was planning to simply put the gun to her own head, why did she need shooting lessons from Ralph Gano, the gun shop owner? Someone planning to shoot herself certainly didn't need multiple lessons in the proper handling of firearms!

Chapter 18

"Connie to Await Fate in Jail Cell"
Indianapolis Star
April 14, 1959

The jury spent just over an hour listening to the complex instructions read by Judge Faulconer before retiring to deliberate. This is a facet of jury trials that the public rarely sees. However, lawyers and judges take it very seriously. An incorrect or leading instruction can skew the verdict in favor of one side or another and cause reversible error that an appellate court may cite in returning the case for a retrial.

Decisions on the instructions were the young judge's last real decisions in the trial and signaled the light at the end of the tunnel. The end was in sight. So far, he had survived.

As happens in most jury trials, neither side was very happy with the instructions. However, the prosecution was especially upset, although the exact reason was unknown. After the instructions were agreed upon by the judge, Thomason called the judge telling him that his selection had "just lost the case for the prosecution." In reality, Thomason was not allowed to even talk to the judge without the other side present. He knew it, too.

No matter how interesting a judge makes the instruction phase, the reading of the instructions is always quite boring and monotonous. In some trials, the reading can go on for a full day or even longer. One of the most common requests juries have is to have the judge repeat one or two of the instructions. Unfortunately, in most jurisdictions, including Criminal Court #2 in 1959, the judge was required to reread all of the instructions. He couldn't read just one or two.

Upon hearing this, without fail, juries opted to skip the rereading of the instructions.

The most important instructions to the jury were those that contained the definitions of first-degree murder, second-degree murder and manslaughter. In a nutshell, the jury was told that first-degree murder required premeditation. Connie would have had to have planned to go to The Meadows, planned to shoot Teel, then carried out the plan.

For second-degree murder, the jury would have to find malice, but not necessarily premeditation. Specifically, they would be required to find that Connie, upon confronting Teel, meant to shoot him, although she may not have planned it in advance.

Manslaughter indicated that no planning took place and the killing occurred in the heat of the moment, or, in legal terms, in the heat of passion. Connie would have had to have killed in a rage.

Judge Faulconer's instructions included two that were quite interesting. He warned the jury very sternly that they were not to find Mrs. Nicholas guilty to set any type of example, a favorite request of prosecutors.

More controversially, he instructed the 12 men to be skeptical of the defendant's statements she allegedly made after her arrest. He reminded them that her statements in the hospital and to reporters were not made under oath and, therefore, should carry less weight in the jurors' minds than the statements she had made under oath in the courtroom.

The prosecution again, was furious, convinced that the judge was losing the case for them.

At 3:30 PM on April 14, 1959, for the first time, the 12 married men of the jury entered the jury room behind the courtroom and didn't reach for the deck of playing cards. Instead, they knew they had a task ahead of them and, like all juries, felt the sooner they got it done, the better.

They were actually better off than most juries today since they had not been sequestered. Court didn't start each day until 9:30 AM and was adjourned most days by 3:30 or 3:45 PM. One common misconception about courts is that they handle one case at a time. Although every judge would like to have that luxury, the other cases have to proceed as well.

Judge Faulconer's docket book shows that he would often conduct proceedings on other cases before and after the Connie Nicholas trial each day.

The shorter hours also afforded the jury some freedom that, indications are, they appreciated. The earlier adjournment gave them the opportunity to go to work for a few hours each afternoon before heading home for the day. Most of them took advantage.

The jury room was plain and nondescript. A rectangular wooden conference table surrounded by chairs was the centerpiece. For the first time, as the jurors filed in single file in numerical order, the bailiffs did not accompany them. Instead, they closed the door behind juror number 12 and stood guard outside.

In the more innocent days of the 1950s, the thought of anyone attempting to intimidate or influence the jury was far from anyone's mind. The newspapers, on two different occasions during the trial, had printed the names, addresses and occupations of each member of the jury.

Still, with one exception, apparently no one attempted to contact the jurors. Juror number 12 did receive a phone call from a woman recommending that he cast his vote a certain way. However, he dismissed it and never mentioned it to his fellow jurors, the judge or other court officials.

The judge, on the other hand, continued to get letters from around the country. He refused to read them. His wife read them after the trial was over. The judge never did.

The first order of business was to elect a foreman. In many jury trials, the foreman is selected because of his or her prior experience on a jury. In this case, no one had any previous history to draw from.

In the end, juror number 7, Russell Cole was selected.

A trial vote was taken to gauge the task that lay ahead. One juror voted for acquittal. One voted for first-degree murder. The other ten were divided between manslaughter and second-degree murder.

This jury was a microcosm of Indianapolis industry. It included an engineer, several factory workers and a postal employee, among others. Because of their backgrounds, they reportedly took the evidence very literally. Each denied that the lifestyle and backgrounds of the defendant and the victim were considered.

The jury first turned to the juror who voted for first degree murder. The others asked him why. He saw little doubt. She took the gun, loaded, to the scene, she shot it four times and killed him. "What else was there to say?" he asked.

This prompted a discussion of the evidence pointing to premeditation. Ultimately, all twelve agreed that there was insufficient evidence of premeditation.

For some reason, they did not consider Connie's trip across town to purchase the gun, the fact the safety was off, the fact she practiced with the gun or, possibly most important, the difficult trigger pull and the spacing of the shots.

Years later, one of the jurors would report that none of that entered their minds as evidence of premeditation.

Another ballot was taken. One acquittal, the rest either manslaughter or second-degree murder.

The jury next turned to the juror who voted for acquittal.

The juror favoring acquittal was the youngest member of the jury. He had just been released from the army and still sported a haircut reminiscent of boot camp. He said that he couldn't really say why, but he felt Connie should be acquitted.

The other jurors peppered him with questions about the evidence and the instructions. Finally, the truth began to come out.

As the youngest member of the famous jury began to tell his story, the other jurors began to wonder if he was consciously chosen by the shrewd defense lawyer Frank Symmes. But, in reality, there was no evidence that anyone in the courtroom had any inkling of the man's past.

It was, indeed, true that he had been discharged recently from the army. However, it was not his idea to leave. The army had thrown him out.

In addition, he went on, he had been involved in a jury "situation" before and, according to him, had been "screwed" by it. He wouldn't elaborate, but most likely, he had been court-martialed.

He then dropped the bombshell, telling the group that since he had been screwed by a jury once, he had vowed to always vote to acquit anyone in a jury trial.

That was his vote. And he didn't plan to change it.

Collectively, the other eleven jurors pushed their chairs across the hard tile floor, away from the table and let out a deep sigh.

This may take longer than they expected.

The vote was now 0 for first-degree murder, 5 for second degree murder, 6 for manslaughter and 1 for acquittal.

During deliberations, the courtroom looked more like pandemonium. Multiple card games were being played throughout the courtroom. Feet were propped on the railing and the attorney's tables. Wives of the lawyers joined the vigil. The judge remained in his chambers, wanting to be close by in the event of a verdict.

This would be a hallmark of Judge Faulconer in later years. He would never leave the courthouse during jury deliberations. He did not want others waiting on him to return from home.

As soon as the jury left the room, Connie was handcuffed by her jail matron, Mildred Lynch, and the two of them, along with a sheriff's deputy made the solemn walk from the courtroom, flanked by the 50 spectators who watched silently as Connie passed. Exiting the courthouse, they walked in the late day sun down the alley and back to the women's jail one block away.

One hour passed without word from the jury.

Jud Haggerty decided to wait it out at home and left.

The men in the jury room began to concentrate on the difference between manslaughter and second-degree murder. The discussion changed the mind of one of the jurors who had originally voted for second-degree murder.

None for first-degree murder, 4 for second-degree murder, 7 for manslaughter and one for acquittal.

Two hours passed.

Evening editions of the newspapers carried stories of the final arguments and predicted a long deliberation. In taverns and across fences, many began predicting manslaughter after Connie's emotional testimony.

Again, none for first-degree murder, 4 for second-degree murder, 7 for manslaughter and one for acquittal.

Three hours passed.

The jury left the courthouse and walked a few blocks to Charlie's Steakhouse for dinner. They returned after one hour and resumed their task.

One more vote was changed. None for first-degree murder, 3 for second-degree murder, 8 for manslaughter and one for acquittal.

It had been four hours.

Just outside the courtroom, a television, black and white, of course, was made available. Many of the participants crowded around to watch news reports of their performance from the day.

Inside the courtroom, the restless crowd, becoming bolder as the evening wore on, began getting noisier. One spectator even went so far as to take the judge's chair on the bench, bang the gavel and begin issuing orders.

The crowd enjoyed the impromptu performance, but when a sheriff's deputy happened in the room, the jokester quickly retreated from the bench. Newspaper reporters tried to interview the man, but he said his name was "Fred" and that was all he could remember.

More progress. None for first-degree murder, 2 for second-degree murder, 9 for manslaughter, one for acquittal.

Five hours. Still no verdict. Still no word from the jury at all.

The door to the jury room could be seen from some vantage points in the courtroom. But a few reporters who went out for some fresh air noticed that you could see three of the jurors through a window from outside. From there on, they watched constantly in shifts, but saw nothing of any consequence.

The last two holdouts for second-degree murder finally gave in to the majority. The vote count was now none for first-degree murder, none for second-degree murder, 11 for manslaughter, one for acquittal. The challenge became convincing the one holdout.

Six hours passed. The night was growing deeper.

The restlessness intensified. Smoke filled the room from cigarettes and cigars. The non-smoking crusade was years away. It was still fashionable to light up.

11 for manslaughter, one for acquittal.

It had been seven hours.

Convincing the lone holdout for acquittal was the difficulty.

11 for manslaughter, one for acquittal.

Eight hours passed.

By now, the courtroom looked like New York City after a ticker tape parade. Cigarette and cigar butts littered the floor, papers, film cans, sandwich wrappers and paper cups littered the tile floor.

Nine hours passed.

Frank Symmes sat alone near the wall smoking a cigar. His wife had formed a Gin Rummy game with a reporter from Life Magazine.

The spectators had each become so distracted by their own activities, that no one heard the bailiff enter the courtroom at 1:48 AM and announce to the attorneys that the jury had reached a verdict. The judge, upon hearing the news, telephoned the jail and ordered Connie returned to hear her fate.

Card games quickly disbanded. Reporters rushed to the telephones to alert their papers that the verdict was forthcoming.

Soon, the court clerk and reporter were back in their seats. All sign of fatigue from the long wait was gone instantaneously. Even those sleeping in and across chairs snapped back to consciousness.

Connie had been waiting patiently, but by her own admission, nervously, for word from the court. With her attorneys still in the courtroom, she sat alone. Awaiting word to stand and hear the verdict, she sat nervously on the side of her prison bed dressed in a slip.

At 1:50 AM, jail matron Mildred Lynch, approached her cell. "Come on, Connie. The jury's back." She hurriedly dressed in the same black outfit she had worn the previous day. She adjusted the feathers in her black hat. Then they left.

"Don't wait up for me," she yelled back to the jail guard with a forced smile.

With the late hour, rather than take the customary walk to the courthouse, a sheriff's station wagon was brought around to take them to the court. Connie, Mildred Lynch and a sheriff's deputy climbed in the car for the short ride.

As the attorneys began reclaiming their seats at the counsel tables, the word spread throughout the crowd that the jury was ready to return and Connie was on her way back from the jail. The media quickly returned to their cameras and recorders. Spectators jockeyed for the front seats vacated by the lengthy intermission.

The gallery in the courtroom waited anxiously. The judge was still not on the bench, the jury was not in the jury box. At 2:15 AM, the door to the left of the judge's bench opened and Connie Nicholas was escorted in by Jail Matron Lynch. She walked quickly to her customary seat, but before sitting down, stared at the empty jury box as her handcuffs were removed.

It was the first time she had entered the courtroom without smiling and acknowledging the media.

She appeared pale and scared. Her makeup appeared to have been applied hurriedly.

Without further warning, the bailiff's words, "All Rise," rang through the courtroom just after Connie was seated. As the crowd rose, the young judge entered through the same door that Connie had passed through moments before. He walked purposefully to the bench, sat down in the high-back red leather chair and announced to the courtroom that everyone may be seated.

With no further explanation, the jury was brought in and filed orderly and silently into the jury box. Connie stared at each one in turn once, then again. None looked back.

One by one, the judge called the jurors by name and number. Each answered with one word, "present."

The silence in the courtroom was absolute.

The judge turned his attention back to the jury box and asked, "Gentlemen of the jury, have you reached a verdict?"

"We have, your honor," responded Foreman Cole.

Typically, the verdict form is handed to the bailiff who passes it directly to the judge without examining it. However, Judge Faulconer surprised everyone by bounding from the bench to the foreman and taking the jury slip himself.

He was so concerned about making a mistake that he had read and reread the law that stated that the judge should receive the verdict from the jury. The law meant that the bailiff would deliver it to the judge, but Faulconer was taking no chances. He was going to literally receive it from the jury.

The quick action of the 230-pound judge caught everyone's attention.

He returned to the bench and opened the folded paper. He read it silently, then shuffled it among some other papers on the desk in front of him.

The wait seemed long to the spectators. It was an eternity to the defendant and her lawyers.

"Will the defendant rise and face the court and jury," he said. Connie stood, looking more scared.

At 2:34 AM on April 15, Judge Faulconer announced the verdict to the court and the defendant.

"We, the jury, find the defendant, Minnie B. Nicholas, alias Connie Nicholas, guilty of voluntary manslaughter."

Connie didn't move. She didn't tremble, flinch or say a word. This was one of the few occasions she didn't cry.

For several seconds the only sound in the courtroom was the flutter of cameras, opening and closing their shutters.

A murmur began to spread through the crowd. "Voluntary manslaughter is 2 to 21 years," the people said to each other. Clearly, some of the trial watchers had done their homework.

And then, it was over.

Frank Symmes asked the court's permission to poll the jury on the slight chance that someone's vote had been misunderstood, coerced or changed. Each reaffirmed his vote for voluntary manslaughter.

Judge Faulconer then announced that he was ready to pronounce sentence on Connie immediately. Frank Symmes asked for a delay of a day or two. The judge set the sentencing for 11:00 AM the next morning.

The judge and Prosecutor Bayt thanked the jury. Then they were dismissed.

With court adjourned for the night, the newsmen surrounded Connie like sharks. Appearing stunned, she whispered to defense attorney Joe Quill, who then said, "She wishes to thank all of you."

Connie had cooperated with the media during the past weeks and months. She had even invited their attention. But now, she simply said that she had no comment. "I just haven't any comment to make."

One reporter asked about an earlier statement saying she would prefer the electric chair to prison. She chose not to respond.

Matron Mildred Lynch stepped forward through the crowd and began to place the handcuffs back on the wrists of the tiny inmate. They left by the same door they had entered.

Chapter 19

"I'm not surprised about anything Judge Faulconer does. He has showed all along he is against me."
Connie Nicholas
November 23, 1959

The jury, released from their civic duties, returned to their homes around 3:30 AM and resumed their normal lives the next day. Although every member of the press knew their name and address, not a single one was contacted for information. Just before alerting the bailiff of their verdict, the 12 men made a pact that they would not discuss what happened in the jury room. When a reporter asked about the verdict as the foreman left the courtroom, he simply said that they took at least 10 ballots and that some were for first-degree murder, some were for acquittal and the rest were in between.

The jury would honor that pact for more than 41 years without exception.

Some didn't like the verdict. Women, in particular, seemed to think voluntary manslaughter was too light. But, conversely, there were others that felt she should have been set free.

In the end, the verdict felt somewhat like a compromise.

And like many jury trials, in a way, it was.

Connie returned to the jail cell, unable to sleep. She refused her breakfast the next morning and frequently asked if Frank Symmes had arrived yet. She was expecting him to come by before the sentencing.

Neither he, nor any other member of the defense team ever came.

At 11:00 AM the next morning, Judge Faulconer once again took the bench of the crowded courtroom, having had time only to return home to take a quick nap, shower and shave. Connie Nicholas, now a convicted felon, was ushered into the courtroom by the sheriff's deputy and the jail matron. The handcuffs were once again removed. Amazingly, the braces on her arms were conspicuously absent at the sentencing.

Connie stood stone-faced as Judge Faulconer sentenced her to a minimum of 2 years and a maximum of 21 years in the Indiana Women's Prison.

Her time in custody in the hospital and in the jail would not count.

Connie seemed quite upset and surprised when Mildred Lynch stepped forward to place the handcuffs back on Connie's wrists. She looked to her lawyers, saying she had expected to be free pending the appeal. She thought she would be going home with her sister.

She was mistaken.

Connie told her attorneys that she had expected to be released on bond that day and was quite surprised that her attorneys had not started the process yet. Frank Symmes told her that they could do that at any time. Connie turned to the young Joe Quill and snapped at him, "I thought you were going to come by this morning."

"I was dead," he responded.

"You got more sleep than I did," she said.

Before being led from the courtroom for the last time, Connie asked for her braces to be placed on her hands. As they began to leave, Mildred Lynch told Connie to slow down so Mildred could straighten her hat. "It doesn't matter now," she replied.

The hat remained crooked, a symbol of her lost pride.

Frank Symmes alerted the court to Connie's intent to appeal and asked the judge to set an appeal bond, a bail bond that allows a convicted felon to go free until the appeal is resolved. The judge set an appeal bond of

$10,000. Charlie Symmes predicted she would be out on bond the following day.

He would be too optimistic.

The sheriff's station wagon left the ancient courthouse at 11:45 AM. By noon Connie was inside the Indiana Women's Prison.

With good behavior, Connie could be eligible for parole after serving 21 months.

However, the judge also sentenced her to pay court costs of $894.65. If she could not pay this, her sentence would be extended by one day for every $5. The court costs alone could increase her sentence by another 6 months.

In essence, court costs and bonds meant little to Connie. She was broke from paying her attorneys. After all, she hadn't been working and the man who supported her was dead. Her attorney fees were less than $5,000.

All was not lost, though. Two local bail bondsmen made a public offer the next morning to post her bond. The offer was hard to decline. The two men, in the admitted pursuit of publicity, were offering the high profile prisoner the bond at no cost, waiving their customary $1,000 fee.

Connie met with the bondsmen and consulted with her attorneys.

She quickly turned it down, to the surprise of many.

While many wondered aloud about Connie's decision to turn down a "get out of jail free card," the fact was that her attorneys had pointed out to her that if she was released, she would be forced to pay for her own food, housing and medical care. And even in the optimistic 50's, she would most certainly incur great difficulty finding employment given her name and uncertain future.

The bondsmen agreed to leave the offer on the table.

Connie's sister, a regular feature at the trial, also reported several phone calls from sympathetic spectators offering to pay all or part of the bond. According to the sister, many of these offers were from people that had never met Connie and only followed the trial long-distance through the press coverage.

She summarily declined these offers as well.

Eventually, Connie accepted the bond from the two bondsmen, finding the lure of freedom too great to resist. At 11:30 AM on Saturday, April 18, 1959, Connie walked from the Indiana Women's Prison and climbed into her sister's waiting car. She notified prison officials that she would be staying with her sister in New Whiteland, a bedroom community close to Indianapolis, pending the outcome of her appeal.

Connie resumed her practice of courting the willing press during her release on bond. Judge Faulconer granted her 30 days in which to make a decision whether to appeal. If she decided to appeal, she would remain free until the appeal was final. If she opted not to appeal, she would have to return to the prison when the 30 days expired.

On Tuesday, April 28, she gave an interview to the Indianapolis Times in which she claimed that prison was "much nicer than I expected." She found the facilities very clean, and the food quite good, deeming it "even better than in General Hospital."

"Now, if they would just move in a swimming pool and a beach, I'd be all set for a vacation," she quipped.

"And, who knows, maybe they'd let me cook a meal for the girls."

The decision of whether to appeal was a difficult one for Connie and her lawyers. The law in the United States was and is that if a defendant is acquitted, she cannot be retried for the same crime again under the Constitutional prohibition against double jeopardy. Practically, this means that the prosecution may not appeal an unfavorable result regardless of the evidence presented. On the other hand, if the defendant is convicted, the defendant may appeal. However, if she wins the appeal, she simply wins a new trial with no guarantee that the new trial will not result in a more harsh verdict and/or sentence. Additionally, a new trial would cause Connie to incur all the attorneys fees, expert fees and other costs a second time.

In considering an appeal, Connie dismissed her trial attorneys and hired two others, two gentlemen with reputations as appellate attorneys. One of the first actions these two attorneys took was to petition Judge Faulconer to declare Connie a pauper. If successful, the state would pay the costs of Connie's appeals of her conviction.

The move also lengthened the time she could remain out on bond.

Judge Faulconer held a hearing on the matter shortly after the motion was filed. In the course of the hearing, it was discovered that, immediately before filing the motion to have herself declared a pauper, she had given her sister title to her car (the 1955 Chevrolet in which she tried to kill herself) and about $1,000.

Based on this discovery, Judge Faulconer summarily refused to grant the petition for a pauper appeal.

Connie, already decrying the job her defense attorneys had done, now turned her wrath to the judge. "I knew Judge Faulconer was out to get me. He has been since the whole case started," she said repeatedly to any media that would listen.

Many did.

It was quickly becoming clear that Connie was blaming everyone but Connie for her predicament. In a jailhouse interview after her conviction, Connie even went so far as to tell the reporter that, although she fired the shots, Betty Teel, Forrest's wife, was at least partly to blame for his death. Apparently rethinking that statement, she refused to elaborate further.

The attorneys appealed Judge Faulconer's ruling denying her pauper status to the Indiana Supreme Court. After several months, the Supreme Court, in a 4 to 0 vote (with one justice not participating), refused to overturn Judge Faulconer's ruling.

Near the end of November, 1959, the bail bondsmen who had given Connie her freedom, decided to revoke her bond. The reason given was that she had begun acting strangely and they were concerned that she would do something that would cause the men to lose the bond they had posted. Specifically, they cited that she had turned on her trial attorneys.

However, many defendants begin questioning the effectiveness of trial counsel. This may have been another publicity stunt.

Judge Faulconer ordered her back to prison just before Thanksgiving, 1959. But within hours, a new bond had been posted and she once again returned to her sister's home. The press questioned the bail bonding company who said only that they had been paid, but did not know by whom. Most likely Connie's sister paid the surety of $1,000 to get the bond.

Connie's appeal took one last gasp. She appealed her conviction, claiming that the jury's finding of manslaughter had been error in the eyes of the law.

She would lose that as well.

Connie's appellate team made overtures to the press that Connie would be appealing her case to the U.S. Supreme Court. But in the end due to the money or perhaps some other reason, that never happened.

In the end, Connie recognized that she had but one real choice. She was broke and, even if she won the appeal, she might be convicted of the same offense, second-degree murder, or even first-degree murder which may cost her her life in the electric chair.

If she could scrape together the $894.65 to pay the court costs and bide her time in the Women's prison for as little as 21 months, she would be free and clear.

The only realistic choice was not to pursue her appeal further, she reluctantly decided.

Finally, almost one year to the day from her conviction, in April, 1960, Connie voluntarily reported to the Women's Prison once more. Her wry sense of humor remained. She requested a private room with a bath.

Ever the ham, Connie told the waiting press that she had decided to return to prison to celebrate another birthday in prison.

With her admission to the building, she began serving her sentence for the voluntary manslaughter of the man she loved.

Indianapolis celebrated the New Year in 1960 in a sorrowful way. Just days after the celebration of a new decade, an entire family of four was killed when the car in which they were riding skidded in front of a bus on its way north to South Bend, Indiana. Nine more died in traffic accidents in the first three days. The same day, 2 brazen bandits robbed one of the finer restaurants on upscale Meridian Street.

The same day, a young, tousle-haired Massachusetts senator named John Kennedy announced that he would be seeking the Democrat nomination for President of the United States.

The papers gave the news of the beginning of the Kennedy political dynasty little space on the front page.

In the most important story from a local perspective, just after midnight on January 2nd, 1960, the dispatcher for the Washington Township Volunteer Fire Department in Indianapolis received an urgent call from a woman who identified herself as Mrs. Florence Stewart. She reported a fire at 6080 Crows Nest Drive.

The home was about as close to an Indianapolis Fire Department station as it was to the fire station in Washington Township, and the dispatcher alerted both the volunteer fire department in Washington Township and the Indianapolis Fire Department.

Within minutes, the normally quiet, residential neighborhood, accessible mainly by one street with little traffic, was awakened by the heart-stopping chorus of multiple sirens and the roar of the powerful diesel engines of the massive red trucks. Bedrooms were illuminated by the spinning red lights as the behemoths passed.

The two-story stone home was far from fully engulfed when the firefighters arrived. The door was unlocked and, after donning the remainder of their safety gear, when they entered the residence, they found the thick, choking smoke confined mainly to the upstairs.

They raced in the front door and directly up the stairs, following the smoke trail to the master bedroom.

Inside the master bedroom, they found little fire, but a tremendous amount of smoke. As they searched the foggy room, they found the bed with a one-foot wide hole in it, still smoldering. A cigarette lighter lay on the smoking bed.

A few steps away, they found the nude body of a woman.

The woman looked to be in her forties, perhaps her early forties. She was found between the bed and the master bathroom. She was alive, but unconscious and badly burned.

The fireman quickly carried the small, limp body from the residence out the front door and to a waiting ambulance. She was taken to Methodist Hospital with second and third degree burns covering more than half of her body.

Unfortunately, this was not the first time the firefighters had been called to this address. Just over three months earlier, they had responded to the report of a fire to find the same woman with serious burns sustained when a cigarette ignited her nightgown. She had spent two weeks in Methodist Hospital and underwent surgery to graft skin on both arms.

Once again, she would make the twenty-five minute trip to Methodist Hospital.

16 year-old Tommy Teel would ride with his mom in the ambulance.

Physicians at Methodist Hospital found that Mrs. Teel was most badly burned on her torso and left thigh. However, they also found burns on her arms, hands and neck. Around daybreak on January 3, after just a few hours in the Hospital, Betty Teel regained consciousness, but was kept under heavy sedation and was in an oxygen tent. Emergency room doctors had given her blood transfusions during the night.

At the same time, firemen returned to the residence to extinguish a flare up in the smoldering mattress dragged to the front yard the night before.

Investigators quickly pieced together the events of the night before.

Betty Teel had, once again, been smoking in bed. Perhaps she fell asleep. Perhaps she had been drinking and had passed out. Whatever the reason, her bathrobe caught fire. She immediately awakened and ran to the bathroom to extinguish the blaze. Fire investigators found ashes from her cigarette in a trail to the bathroom sink.

On her way back to the bed, she collapsed.

The flaming bathrobe had done its damage. The pain was too great. Her body gave up and slipped into unconsciousness.

In the meantime, hot ashes from the cigarette and the bathrobe smoldered on and in the mattress filling the upstairs of the fashionable home with smoke.

Tommy Teel had been attending a school dance and returned home around midnight. Upon opening the front door, he smelled and saw the smoke. He ran back to his car and drove to the house of the nearest neighbor that he knew, a few blocks away. The neighbor alerted the authorities.

Over the next few days, her condition officially remained unchanged. The press was told, simply, she was in critical condition.

However, two days after being brought to the hospital, the short, tragic life of Mary Elizabeth "Betty" Teel was over.

She died at 12:30 PM, Wednesday, January 6, 1960.

Her funeral was held January 8 at the same mortuary where her husband had lain 18 months earlier.

The ceremony, much like the victim, was private.

Young Tommy Teel spent the next two years living with relatives in Texas. After completing high school in Texas, he opted to remain there.

He was a resident of Texas until his death. He died of natural causes. He was only in his 50s.

Chapter 20

"Happy Connie Free After Prison Term"
Headline,
The Indianapolis News
April 4, 1962

Connie Nicholas was eligible for parole after just 21 months. She had paid her court costs and, she believed, her debt to society.

The parole board didn't agree.

During her incarceration, Connie was assigned to the task of taking the booking pictures of incoming inmates.

To the dismay of many who believed that Connie deserved much more time, she was paroled just months later on April 4, 1962.

The Indiana Women's Prison could have been mistaken for a college or university. It was a small complex of dark, brick buildings separated by brick walkways and settled amid tall maple and oak trees. The trees were trimmed so that their lowest branches were ten or more feet above the ground, but the thick canopy they formed had reduced the ground beneath to bare dirt. Grass wouldn't grow in the heavy shade.

Connie walked from the prison building into the cold, crisp morning air, leaving the chain link fencing at exactly 8:21 AM. She wore a new brown suit and carried a tan travel bag. She had awakened at 4:00 AM that morning, "excited, you know," as she put it. She wore heavy eye makeup. Tears welled in her eyes as she approached the world she had left behind almost two years ago. The tears gave way to sobs.

Despite her indiscretions and crime, despite her lifelong brand as a convicted felon, Connie still evoked sympathy among many. Workers at the prison rushed to her side, placed their arms around her shoulders and encouraged her. "Don't cry now, Connie."

That probably made it worse.

As the gate swung closed behind her, Connie faced the 12 reporters gathered to get their first glimpse of the infamous Connie Nicholas in months. She managed a smile through her sobs. "It looks like old home week, doesn't it?" she said.

She had lost a few pounds and prison seemed to have taken some of the sparkle from her eyes. Relief now took its place.

After a few steps she opened the door of the white Buick belonging to her sister Mabel and Mabel's husband. Connie quickly opened the back door of the sedan, tossed her bag inside and climbed into the front seat.

The car, already running, left the drive of the prison without stopping.

"Good luck," said one reporter quietly as the car disappeared from view.

That was the last Indianapolis saw of Minnie Bell "Connie" Nicholas.

Although the president of Lilly in the late 1950s was not a member of the Lilly family, with a family member on the board and the well-known history of the company, there was little doubt who was ultimately in charge. The executives with the company had developed a habit of flaunting their success, much to the dismay of the Lilly family who preferred to keep their wealth quiet, only grabbing attention through philanthropic endeavors. One of the favorite status symbols for the top executives was a white Cadillac. All of the vice-presidents and others at Lilly had chosen white Cadillacs as their automobile of choice.

As the torrid details of the life of Forrest Teel were made public, an order was made from the chairman of the board through the president. First, anyone who was maintaining a similar lifestyle to Forrest Teel, should stop right now. Second, get rid of the white Cadillacs.

Some traded their cars for other, less conspicuous status symbols. Others simply painted over the white factory finish.

To this day, rumors abound that Lilly even paid to repaint the cars, but that may or may not be true.

Even now, Lilly employees old enough to remember, don't discuss the Forrest Teel murder, considered by the Lilly family to be a black mark in the company's history.

The murder of Forrest Teel also illustrates the change in the world in the last half of the 1900s. In 1950, Indianapolis had one operational television station. Today, murder and other violent crimes are shown nightly on dramas and "reality" television shows on any one of over 100 channels. Most telling, perhaps, is the fact that today's "entertainment" consists of a hearty display of nudity and sexual overtones. During one of the most sensational "sex" trials of the 1950s, the word "sex" was never once uttered in the courtroom and rarely in the newspapers. Witnesses talked of "visits" and "dates." Everyone knew what was going on. No further explanation was required or given.

Today, all the lurid details are required—and expected.

One thing that hasn't changed is the attitude of some areas of the country to allowing media coverage of courtroom proceedings. Certainly, some jurisdictions allow it, there are even cable television channels that broadcast from courtrooms on a daily basis. Yet, an equal number, including the federal courts, cling steadfast to the proposition that press and justice don't mix.

One must ask, what are they afraid of?

The Connie Nicholas trial showed that such coverage can be afforded and managed without deterioration of a defendant's rights.

The Connie Nicholas trial made several "ordinary" people famous, some for a day or two, some for longer periods. Ultimately, one of the most reluctant celebrities was the woman who started it all. Connie Nicholas served her debt to the State of Indiana and was released from the Women's Prison. During her trial, she had told the media that if she were acquitted, she would change her name and try to slip back into anonymity. Upon her release, she decided that that course of action might still be a good idea.

When the gates opened and Connie stepped out, she found several members of the fourth estate ready to update the still curious public on her life. Within a few weeks, Connie would successfully petition a court for a legal name change and slip into the anonymity she claimed to want taking up residence in the small community of New Whiteland, about 15 miles south of Indianapolis.

She must have made up with at least one of the trial attorneys she had previously blamed for her conviction. The petition for her name change was filed by Joe Quill.

A few members of her new community knew who the infamous woman with the unknown name was, but no one ever betrayed her. To this day, the residents of the town refuse to talk about their infamous resident. The press never caught up with her again and eventually, lost interest in her. Several members of the community who know her do profess that she is still alive. She would now be in her 80's.

In a way, Laura Mowrer suffered the same fate. Quickly after the murder of her new boyfriend, Forrest Teel, literally in her front yard, the pretty little 29 year-old fled to California to, successfully, escape the coverage and salvage her reputation.

It worked.

A few years later, when the country had moved onto other interests, Laura reportedly returned quietly to the

Indianapolis area. She married and has lived her life in the obscurity she so highly valued in 1958.

She is also reportedly still alive, living in central Indiana. She would be in her early 70s. With the passage of time and an almost certain name change with her marriage, pretty, young Laura simply disappeared.

Many of the other characters in this tragic drama have not fared as well. Of the three members of the prosecution team, none is alive. Philip Bayt died in 1989 at the age of 79. Chief Deputy Prosecutor Francis Thomason died in the 1970s. Young Jud Haggerty, just 34 at the time of the trial, spent a life in the legal community in Indianapolis. Along the way, he also served as a Marion County public defender and was very active in Democrat politics in Indiana. He was president of the Marion County Young Democrats. Prior to the Connie Nicholas trial, he served in the Indiana House of Representatives from 1949 to 1950, the youngest person to have been elected to that body. Jud Haggerty retired in 1996 after 45 years in the law. He died in 1997 at the age of 72.

The wily, shrewd defense lawyer Frank Symmes would never again have such an important case or client. He continued to work until his death a few years later.

His son, Charles Symmes, became an icon in Indianapolis legal circles as a principal in the leading criminal defense law firm in Indianapolis. Although in his later years, he restricted his practice to business and estate matters, he had the foresight to recruit and train some of the best criminal defense lawyers in Indiana. One of these was James Voyles, the local attorney chosen to assist with the defense of boxer Mike Tyson in 1992. Indeed, many local observers and legal experts believed the outcome would have been quite different had Tyson hired Voyles instead of trusting his defense to his higher-priced, higher-profile Washington, D.C. lawyers.

Shortly after the Connie Nicholas trial, Symmes developed a passion for running that would last the rest of his life. In 1999 and 2000, he was the oldest runner in the Indianapolis Mini-Marathon, an annual 13.1 mile race through the streets of Indianapolis, including a lap around the famous Indianapolis Motor Speedway.

Just two weeks after the 2000 Mini-Marathon, after a short day at work, Symmes returned to his home and took his customary evening run. Less than 100 feet from his house, the 82 year-old Symmes suffered a heart attack and succumbed in the arms of his wife.

Joe Quill remains a practicing attorney in Indianapolis.

In one of the more ironic twists concerning the aftermath of the Forrest Teel murder, the pathologist who performed the autopsy, Dr. Emmett Pierce, was recruited just a few years later to work for a pharmaceutical corporation that maintained 13 research beds in General Hospital. The company was Eli Lilly. He remained there until his retirement in 1986. He and his wife had eight children and still live in Indianapolis.

The Marion County Courthouse was also a casualty. During the Connie Nicholas trial, the city approved plans and financing for a new City-County Building. It was erected over a period of two years directly behind the old Courthouse. The modern steel and glass structure became home to all offices for Marion County and the City of Indianapolis, including all Marion County Courts.

Upon the opening of the new City-County Building in 1962, demolition on the historic courthouse began.

My father, Judge Faulconer may have fared the best of anyone involved in the trial. Although he would never again preside over a trial involving such intense public and media interest and curiosity, the reputation that he gained through his near flawless handling of the Connie Nicholas trial would vault him to prominence in state politics. In 1963, when an elected judge on the Indiana Appellate Court died mid-term, Governor Matthew Welsh appointed Faulconer to the Court of Appeals to serve out the decedent's term.

He would be elected to the Indiana Court of Appeals for a full term in 1964, serving as the chief judge of the Court. In 1968, the Democrats in Indiana nominated him as a candidate for one of the five justices on the Indiana Supreme Court. In a Republican landslide behind President Richard Nixon, Faulconer lost.

In 1970, he was again nominated for Judge of the Indiana Court of Appeals, losing by only 476 votes out of nearly two million votes cast. It is the closest statewide election in Indiana history.

Soon, the federal court system tapped him and he was appointed as the Chief U.S. Magistrate for the Southern District of Indiana. He served in that position for 16 years.

All told, when he retired in 1986, Judge Faulconer had 25 years on the bench in Indiana.

He remains retired and continues to live in Indianapolis, Indiana. With his wife of almost 50 years, they have reared four children. Unfortunately, his fondness of Milky Way candy bars and butterscotch milkshakes, along with his abhorrence of exercise have taken their toll. A diabetic for over thirty years, his eyesight is rapidly failing as a result. After a mild heart attack, he was fitted with a pacemaker. However, his heart has continued to weaken and he now suffers from congestive heart failure.

He is still an outspoken proponent of cameras in courtrooms.

About the Author

Tom Faulconer is an attorney, Certified Financial Planner and the Director of Marketing Training for Farm Bureau Insurance, headquartered in Indianapolis, Indiana.

He is a frequent lecturer to insurance and financial professionals on topics involving taxation, business organizations and ethics. In addition, he conducts seminars for the public designed to help individuals understand the complexities of business, tax and insurance planning in an entertaining way.

Tom is an adjunct faculty member of the School of Business at Butler University, his alma mater, as an instructor of commercial and business law and risk management. Previously he was a member of the adjunct faculty at Indiana University-Purdue University at Indianapolis where he was voted the Schuyler F. Otteson Award for teaching excellence, an honor awarded by vote of the student body.

Tom is known for his ability to take complex topics and make them concise and understandable. This manuscript reflects his fascination with the extraordinary events that beset ordinary people.

He is a lifelong resident of the Indianapolis area where he lives with his wife and son.

Printed in the United States
705000001B